The Ulti
Guide to Editing
Your Novel

The Ultimate Guide to Editing Your Novel

A REVOLUTIONARY APPROACH TO TRANSFORM YOUR WRITING

by Sara Grant

BLOOMSBURY YEARBOOKS

LONDON • OXFORD • NEW YORK • NEW DELHI • SYDNEY

BLOOMSBURY YEARBOOKS
Bloomsbury Publishing Plc
50 Bedford Square, London, WC1B 3DP, UK
Bloomsbury Publishing Ireland Limited
29 Earlsfort Terrace, Dublin 2, D02 AY28, Ireland

BLOOMSBURY YEARBOOKS, WRITERS' & ARTISTS'
and the Diana logo are trademarks of Bloomsbury Publishing Plc

First published in Great Britain 2025
This edition published 2025

A catalogue record for this book is available from the British Library

ISBN: 9781399418867; eBook: 9781399419154

2 4 6 8 10 9 7 5 3 1

Design by Catherine Lutman Design
Printed and bound in Great Britain by CPI Group (UK) Ltd, Croydon CRO 4YY

To find out more about our authors and books visit www.bloomsbury.com and sign up for our
newsletters. For product safety related questions contact productsafety@bloomsbury.com

Contents

INTRODUCTION

You've finished a draft of your novel. Now what?

First, congratulations! I've met so many amazing writers who never manage to commit a beginning, middle and end to the page. Completing a rough draft is an outstanding feat of imagination and resilience. But it's only the start of your journey to publication. The difference between a good novel and a publishable one is a rigorous revision process. Reading and re-reading your draft from start to finish just isn't enough.

My systematic approach will revolutionise how you think about revision. This step-by-step system was developed over my many years as an editor, author, university lecturer and mentor. Because of my background in writing and editing books for children and young adults, this workbook includes additional content on the responsibilities and challenges unique to writing for young readers.

How to use this book

This is a practical, how-to guide. The exercises are straightforward and, with some thought and hard work, they will transform your manuscript. I've laid it out as a workbook with the expectation that you'll move from start to finish, addressing the different elements of your novel in turn; you can't revise every aspect of a novel all at once. You will review your manuscript in a number of different ways, and at each stage you may want to apply what you've learned throughout your novel. This may mean you write several drafts before you finally have the one that is ready to send to agents and editors or to self-publish.

The first step is solidifying your vision for the novel. What novel did you set out to write? Why are you writing it and why are you the only one who can tell this story? Your answers to these questions will guide you throughout your revision process. It's easy to let demanding characters take over or to be enchanted by new and shiny ideas that shift the focus of your draft. Once you've honed your vision, keep it at the heart of your revision.

The next and more complex challenge is to discover what you've actually captured on the page. First, you'll interrogate your idea. Then you will scrutinize the plot, characters, setting and voice of your story. Ultimately, you'll review your manuscript chapter by chapter, scene by scene, sentence by sentence and, finally, word by word.

Along the way I will offer some guidelines. Of course, it's possible to find (and your work may reflect) exceptions to these guidelines. One of the cornerstones of my revision process is what I call conscious creation: know when your work is outside the norm. When you disregard the guidelines, do so for good reason and because it's the best way to tell your story.

This workbook contains a series of exercises and interrogations to uncover areas of excellence and opportunities for improvement. This approach helps you control the story on the page and in the minds of your readers. Not every exercise will resonate with you, and that's fine.

Every writer has different challenges. Some know how to hook the reader from the opening page but lose steam and focus as the draft wears on. Others are masters at page-turning plots, but their characters are mere cardboard cut-outs. Some effortlessly create authentic, sparky characters that demand our attention but lead us nowhere, while others conjure an atmosphere and a sensory experience but little else. And then there's that very rare writer who has commanded hook, voice, character, plot, atmosphere and setting but needs help with the final polish. I encourage you to experiment with the exercises in the chapters that follow. You may be surprised at what unlocks the next draft or inspires a new and improved direction for your writing and your story.

You also can use this book as a diagnostic tool. Maybe you already know what's not working in your novel. You have plot problems or 'flat' characters, for example. You can dip in and out of the chapters that focus on these issues.

My aim was to create a resource that you can use time and time again. My favourite quote for my life and my writing comes from the late, great Maya Angelou: 'Do the best that you can until you know better. Then when you know better, do better.' Eventually I hope you assimilate this editorial approach so that each subsequent novel takes less time and energy to revise.

Are you ready to transform your draft? Open your manuscript on your computer or print out a copy. Grab some highlighters and your caffeine of choice and let's go!

CHAPTER I

Interrogating your idea

This chapter lays the foundation for your revision. I'll ask some big questions about you and your book. Your answers will serve as your North Star throughout the revision process. I've included a few exercises to help you take a bird's-eye view of your novel. I end the chapter with a discussion of the challenges when writing for children. If this is your aim, I've included a few additional questions to ensure that what you are writing is, in fact, a novel for young children, teens or young adults.

When writers who might be stuck at the start of a novel, drowning in the murky middle or unable to create a satisfying ending, ask me how I manage to write mine, I explain that I allow myself to write a terrible first draft. No, I mean it! I don't worry that every word is the exact right one. (I will do that later, though.) At this stage, I couldn't care less about spelling, grammar or punctuation. All I want is to translate my idea into a manuscript with a beginning, middle and end. In my experience, you need to finish a draft of a novel to find out what it's really about. Plot, characters and themes often reveal themselves along the way. When we allow ourselves the freedom to explore and play in the first draft, we often write our way into a wonderful story.

Using my systematic approach to revision, I can transform my terrible first draft into a publishable story. My current work-in-progress is a contemporary story for middle-grade readers. It's roughly 40,000 words. Because I'm interested in the process of writing, I decided to track my time. So far I've spent 220 hours writing the book. Approximately 30 per cent of that time was writing the first draft; a whopping 70 per cent was spent revising.

So don't worry if your first draft is really rough. I'm here to help.

The first of our big questions is:

Why do you feel compelled to tell this story?

In *101 Habits of Highly Successful Screenwriters*, Akiva Goldsman says:

> The trick is to be connected to the material of your imagination, thematically and concretely. Write what interests you, because if you're not fascinated and excited by the writing of the script, the reader won't be fascinated and excited by the reading of it. Try to find something in the idea that speaks to your own life, something you think is authentic and true and compelling in the story you want to tell.

That's what I call the **intention** of your novel. Some call it heart. Your story needs an angle or vision, a way of looking at the world, that's your own: fresh, original and deeply felt. That's what the first big question is about.

The stronger your passion for the story, the more likely you'll be to finish it and the more likely that your readers will feel this heart beating on every page. I'm not asking you to write down the plot or your enthusiasm for one of your characters. Not why you are interested or motivated or curious about the story – but why *must* you write it?

If you've finished your draft and it's falling flat, maybe it's because it lacks this sort of energy and intention. Having an intention – and remaining true to it – can be what makes a good book great.

For some, the heart of the story is its theme. (We'll talk more about theme in Chapter 3.) You have an important topic you want to explore. For others, it's the genre – they've always wanted to write a mystery or romance or action adventure. Maybe you want to make children laugh or you want to share a universal experience so they don't feel so alone. All are great reasons to write.

Some authors write for young readers because they want to teach them something. This comes from a good place. We want our readers to have an easier time than we did growing up. But don't write to educate. Children and teens can spot a lesson a mile away. Issues must be handled subtly in the story. Let your message bubble up from the story and the characters. Let your readers discover it, not be *told* it. Don't write *for* children; write as if you are a child/teen. Write authentic and true stories from a young person's perspective.

For me, writing has always been a mix of imagination and exploration. When I was a teen, I wrote poetry to explore my feelings and organize my thoughts. I enjoy writing stories that allow me to ponder big questions. I don't write because I have the answers, but because I'm interested in the questions. I want my novels to be conversation-starters. I don't want to tell readers what they should think and feel; I want to give them the space to explore. In my debut young adult novel *Dark Parties*, I wanted to demonstrate the power of diversity. In *Half Lives*, my second young adult novel, I was interested in religion and wondered how, in the future, an ordinary teen might be worshipped as a god. And my current work-in-progress explores how we form our opinions and why it's okay to agree to disagree.

But my first responsibility as a children's author is to entertain my readers. If they don't turn the page, I will never be able to have a conversation about important ideas.

The next big question is:

Why are *you* the only one who can tell this story?

Often writers are observers, bystanders. We watch and listen and learn about human nature. When I ask writers this question, they often struggle with an answer. They aren't sure what makes them special, qualified or unique enough to tell this story.

The good news is … we are all original. I'm from southern Indiana in the United States. Growing up, I struggled with giving myself permission to tell stories. I was just an average child. Surely I wasn't special enough? What did I know?

A hell of a lot, as it turns out.

We all have a unique way of looking at the world. Trust in your uniqueness. What original perspective will you bring to the story?

Remain true to your vision

Keep your responses to these two big questions at the heart of your revision: Why do you feel compelled to tell the story? and Why are you the only one who can tell it? You may need to change plot, characters, setting, etc., but know why you are compelled to tell this story and remain true to it throughout the revision process.

I accepted an offer from Little, Brown on *Dark Parties* not because the editor thought I was a genius and didn't want me to change one single word, but because she identified what *wasn't* working. She helped me address those issues and made *Dark Parties* a better book. One of the final changes my editor suggested was to consider if the book could have a more ambiguous ending. She felt I'd wrapped up the story too neatly.

One of the reasons I wrote *Dark Parties* was to immortalize my beloved late grandma. The protagonist is searching for her missing grandma. Not to get too philosophical, but I wasn't sure if I'd ever be reunited with my grandma, so very much wanted Neva, the protagonist, to be reunited with hers at the end of the book. Because I knew the answers to these big questions, I knew that there was no way I could honour my editor's request.

I wrote a three-page email expressing why, personally and professionally, I could not make the change my editor wanted. I rewrote the ending a bit and changed one – important – full stop to a question mark. But I needed the reunion between grandma and granddaughter to remain the final moment in the book. I spent hours crafting the message and was absolutely terrified. It was my debut novel, and I didn't want to do anything to ruin the great relationship I had with my editor. I pressed *Send* and held my breath …

My editor's response was quick:

Thank you for your thoughtful explanation. Of course, this is your book, and I definitely understand where you're coming from. I think your revised ending is great – it strikes the right tone. I think we have a winner! Done and done. Onward!

To quote my lovely editor, onward!

Exercise

Your inspiration

If you've struggled to respond to these first two questions, this exercise might help.

Name three books that moved you when you were the age of your protagonist:

1. _____

2. _____

3. _____

Analyse why you loved these books. Is there a common denominator – a theme or style, perhaps?

How can your book offer the same experience to readers?

Read for inspiration

I always recommend reading books for the same age and in the same genre as the story you are trying to write – at every stage of the process. I never trust writers who say they don't read children's books but are trying to write one. I've also heard writers say they are afraid that reading for inspiration while writing their own story will unduly influence them and might make them mimic other writers. I read in the hope that I *will* be positively influenced by great writers. The more you fill your brain with great writing, the more likely you are to produce it.

Big picture analysis

Now we move from the philosophical to the practical. The next series of questions and exercises are designed to help you pinpoint significant aspects of your story that may need adjustments.

Is it a story?

You may think that this is a simple one. But stories are more than having a beginning, a middle and an end. In his brilliant book *Revision and Self-Editing for Publication*, James Scott Bell offers this deceptively simple Fiction Formula:

$$\text{Concept} + \text{Character} \times \text{Conflict} = \text{Novel}$$

Let's test your novel with Bell's Fiction Formula.

Bell defines, 'Concept is the big idea, the basic premise, the one-liner that will explain your story.' Sometimes expressed in a *what would happen if … ?* statement.

Examples of concept:

- What would happen if two girls on holiday follow a rainbow and discover a fairy who needs their help? Answer: *Rainbow Magic*
- What would happen if in eighteenth-century London, an heiress and a girl whose family owns a tea shop see something suspicious during a play and realise they must prevent a murder? Answer: *The Lizzie and Belle Mysteries: Drama and Danger*
- What would happen if a poor boy found a golden ticket for an exclusive tour of the world's most amazing chocolate factory? Answer: *Charlie and the Chocolate Factory*
- What would happen if a 16-year-old girl takes her younger sister's place in a deadly game of survival that's broadcast live to a dystopian world? Answer: *The Hunger Games*

What is the concept of your novel?

Can you write the concept of your story in a simple one-liner?

Do you have a compelling protagonist?

Of course you have a main character, but is she/he/they intriguing enough to entice us to read your novel from the opening paragraph to the bitter and brilliant end? We will spend an entire chapter on developing your character more fully, but for now a little quick test.

In *Revision and Self-Editing for Publication*, Bell notes that great characters have three things: 1) grit, 2) wit and 3) it.

- According to Bell, 'Grit is guts in action'.

- You probably understand what wit is: a warm, natural humour.

- And finally *it* – that spark, that something special about your character.

Bell's definition of great characters always makes me think of Mattie Gokey from Jennifer Donnelly's Carnegie award-winning novel, *A Gathering Light* (*A Northern Light* in the original US edition). Mattie is a lover of words and a solver of mysteries who is determined to chase her dream despite mounting odds. I also adore the lively, number-loving Anisha Mistry in Serena Patel's *Anisha, Accidental Detective*. And who can forget the hysterically dramatic Noah Grimes in *Noah Can't Even* by Simon James Green?

So what's special about your main character?

And finally … the conflict! In life we try to avoid it, but on the page we need it. Defined simply, conflict is the main problem facing your protagonist. A few examples:

- In Ashley Thorpe's *The Boy to Beat the Gods*, the protagonist Kayode must battle a series of gods to save his younger sister.
- Each book in the *Beast Quest* series finds Tom and Elenna freeing a beast.
- The main conflict in Stephanie Meyer's *Twilight* ignites when mere mortal Bella falls in love with a vampire.

What's the main conflict in your story?
Your story must have all three elements in Bell's formula – interesting concept, great characters and conflict. If you had difficulty responding to any of these questions, they may point to what needs attention in your novel. Don't worry, the rest of this book will help you figure out any problems you identify.

There's a line in Karl Iglesias' *Writing for Emotional Impact* that perfectly sums up what makes a great idea: 'A great idea should be uniquely familiar, and it should promise conflict.'

You've noted the main conflict in your story above. Check! Now consider whether it's *uniquely familiar*. I love this phrase. It defines ideas that connect with all of us, universal experiences that transcend time but have a twist that's new and fresh.

Is your idea uniquely familiar? if so, how?

Exercise

Quick outline

Another quick check of your story is what's known as the Pixar Story Structure. It's from the genius animators who brought us *Toy Story, Coco, Ratatouille* and my personal favourite, *Up*.

The Pixar Story Structure is the ability to tell your story in seven sentences. Let's see if you have a Pixar pitch:

1. Once upon a time _____.

2. Every day _____.

3. But one day _____.

4. Because of that _____.

5. Because of that _____.

6. Until finally _____.

7. And ever since then _____.

I tried this for the first book in my *Magic Trix* series.

Once upon a time there was a funny and kind 9-year-old who dreamt of being special.

Every day Trixibelle Morgan wants to believe in magic and wishes she had a cat. Her shy best friend Holly wants to be a magician.

But one day on her tenth birthday, Trix thinks she sees a witch flying across the full moon with a cat on the back of her broomstick.

Because of that she discovers she has the gift of magic and is invited to secretly train to be a fairy godmother. (Only the best and brightest witches become fairy godmothers.)

Because of that she receives an invisible kitten as her magical spirit animal and must keep her magic and the kitten a secret from Holly and her family.

Until finally Trix learns to control her powers and gives Holly the confidence to perform a magic trick at the school talent show – granting her wish like a real fairy godmother.

And ever since then Trix believes in herself and is one step closer to being a real fairy godmother.

This basic outline may not work for every plot, but I like doing a quick check like this with my draft to see if there's a story that I can shape.

How is your story original?

We've already established that you and only you can write this story. You've determined why it's so important to you, now we want to make sure that you can articulate how it is original.

At some point when you are writing a novel, I guarantee you will start to see versions of your idea everywhere. Just as I finished *Dark Parties*, which was about a country that had closed its borders under an electrified dome, I visited a bookshop and spotted a book titled *Under the Dome* – by bestselling behemoth Stephen King, no less! My heart sank. I could barely bring myself to pick up the gorgeous hardback and read the blurb. Even though my book was under contract, certainly that meant my publisher would kill my book deal. I mean, Stephen King had written a book with a dome – in the way that only Stephen bloody King can.

And I was right. Not about my publisher, but about the book. Stephen King had written about a dome in his own brilliant way. His story was nothing like mine. Our books both had domes, but our ideas had rocketed off in wholly different directions.

Exercise

The pitch

Often writers wait until they finish their book to write the pitch. I usually write the pitch as I'm developing my outline and writing the first chapter. Sometimes it is the first thing I write, because it helps crystallize my idea. Writing a pitch as you start your revision can help really nail what you are trying to accomplish and will make it easier to streamline your novel. Also if you can pitch your book in a line or two, it has a better chance of finding a publisher.

There are many ways to pitch your novel. Here are five different techniques to try out, or to use in combination with each other. These are based on an exercise that my writer/editor, colleague and friend Sara O'Connor developed for a retreat we organized for a few years. Experiment with all of them until you find what works for you.

1. **X is Y until Z**[*]

    X = Character

    Y = Circumstances

    Z = Inciting Incident

Let's take an example from a well-known series: Harry Potter is the orphan forced to live under the stairs until he discovers he is a wizard and is whisked away to Hogwarts, a boarding school for wizards. Another example comes from the series *My Sister the Vampire*: cheerleader Olivia is nervous at her new school until she bumps into a gothy vampire girl who turns out to be the twin sister she never knew she had.

---

[*]   Technique from **www.JohnMCusick.com** via **kathytemean.wordpress.com**.

2. The film pitch: X meets Y

Combine well-known references – books, TV shows, and most often films, though not overused ones. Know who you will be pitching to, and pick points of reference they will know and understand. My editor at Little, Brown pitched *Dark Parties* as *1984* meets *Handmaid's Tale*. It's also effective to compare two unexpected references. Don't, for instance, pitch *Star Wars* meets *Star Trek*. Yes, I know they are very different, but the pairing is not surprising. A better example is *Bake Off* meets Pokémon Go. But you'll have to follow up with a quick sentence to show why that comparison makes sense for your story.

I had an early draft of a novel that wasn't coming together. The idea was inspired by the film *Little Miss Sunshine* and set in that horrible world of toddler beauty pageants. Writing a film-style pitch sorted out my plot problem. I realized – as strange as this may sound – it was *Little Miss Sunshine* meets *The Manchurian Candidate*. Yes, it was that bizarre, but this second reference gave me a place to look for inspiration. I watched the film and found the intersections with my story, which helped with figuring out my plot.

3. The *for* pitch

With this pitch style, you find a book, film or TV series reference that is similar to your book, but you have put your unique spin on the idea *for* the age range of your targeted readers. For example, I pitched my *Chasing Danger* series as *Charlie's Angels* for tweens. It perfectly captured the girl power and action-adventure vibe in the series. Make sure that the age groups are contrasting enough to make sense, but are not too unbelievable – no *Hunger Games* for toddlers, for example.

4. The core problem/idea

This type of pitch is the most difficult, because it can easily get bogged down in plot. You can end up summarizing what happens in your story instead of pitching. If the idea – or concept – is so amazing that you have to have it in your pitch, it must be brief. A good example of this type of pitch is Patrick Ness' *Knife of Never Letting Go*. His story is set in a world where everyone can hear everyone else's thoughts *all the time*. Here's another example for *Dinosaur Club* (originally titled *Dinosaur Cove*), a series for young readers: Two young boys find a secret cave that leads to a world of real, live dinosaurs.

5. The premise

Articulate the premise for your story as defined by Robert McKee. If you don't have a copy of McKee's *Story*, it's a great resource. Premise is an open-ended question that your story will answer. What would happen if ...

- a young witch trained to be a fairy godmother, as my series *Magic Trix* asked?
- you save your goldfish's life but accidently make him a zombie goldfish? Mo O'Hara's *My Big Fat Zombie Goldfish* provides the answer.
- a country closed its borders to people and ideas? Find out by reading my book *Dark Parties*.

Write down your pitch in one sentence, using whatever pitch technique works best. Keep it simple.

Once you have your pitch, test it out on people, especially on writer friends if you have them. What questions do they have? Do their eyes light up or glaze over?

My final question on your pitch is: **does your idea feel surprising in some way?** You want your pitch to prompt good questions, not confusion. Does it feel surprising and inspiring? If so, you may have a winner.

Writing for young readers

Is it a story for children, teens or young adults?

Many of the exercises I share in this book can be used for novels of any length, for any age and for any genre. My experience as an editor, writer and lecturer has focused primarily on books for children, teens and young adults. This section considers some additional challenges when writing for readers younger than you.

It's helpful to understand how the market is segmented. I'm never sure that I agree with age bands for readers. Readers don't progress at the same rate: many can read at a higher level while others take more time. I never want to put off a reader because the book is listed as too young or too old for them. Still, this is roughly how the industry – publishers and booksellers – organise books:

Young fiction

Early readers – These are typically reading schemes with prescribed vocabulary.

5+ – These short, highly illustrated chapter books are for readers who are starting to read independently.

7+ – These longer books, typically with a few black-and-white illustrations, are aimed at readers who can read independently.

Middle grade

Middle-grade books are generally for 9 to 12 year-olds. The reading ability in this age range can vary greatly. Some publishers and booksellers break this category into younger middle grade and tween.

Young adult

These stories are for readers aged 13 and older.

All the same rules apply for writing a story for any age. You need:

- memorable characters
- an engaging plot
- an interesting setting
- and, as in all good books, an authentic voice and creative spark.

The added responsibility of writing for children

When non-writers find out I write for children, sometimes I'm asked when I'll graduate to writing for adults. Argh! Writing for children is an honour and privilege. You help young readers learn to navigate the world and become the adults they want to be. Your book might be the first romance or mystery they've ever read. You might open their eyes to issues or topics they've never thought of before. If we do it well, writing for children looks deceptively easy.

In addition to writing an engaging story, we also have a duty of care. We owe it to young readers and their parents to be responsible with what we share. I'm definitely not suggesting you should avoid difficult subjects, but do so thoughtfully and supportively. Think long and hard about what you are exploring with young readers.

Over ten years ago, I was on a book tour in the United States promoting my book *Half Lives*. It focuses on an apocalyptic event by following one of the survivors. During my school presentation, we discussed students' visions of the future. At one point I asked students to raise their hands if they thought we'd be better or worse off in the future. I was shocked when every time, only one or two students believed the world would be better. They saw my story as prophetic. Even though my story was hopeful, it was feeding into their dismal view of the future. I'm an optimist and typically see the best in people. I'm hopeful about tomorrow. After this reaction from readers, I wasn't sure I'd write another dark, dystopian tale – and am still not.

In addition to supporting our readers, we also must understand them: their level of vocabulary, their life experiences, their understanding of the world. Some new writers make the mistake of writing in the style of the books that captured their imagination when they were young. Don't! Times have changed. Childhood has changed. The world has changed. Write from the universal experience of being a child/teen, but if you are writing contemporary fiction, do your research – as you would if you were writing historical fiction. Today's young people experience the world differently than we did. Respect, understand and embrace this exciting new world. Understand how school, technology and a multitude of other things have changed since you were a child. Any reference more than two years old could feel outdated to your readers.

This extra effort will be richly rewarded. Young readers have a unbridled passion for books and authors that most adults don't. I love visiting schools and sharing my passion for books and creative writing with students. It's as close as I'll ever get to my rock star moment – walking across a playground with children shouting my name and asking for my autograph.

What exactly is a children's book?

The definition can be blurry. When I was teaching the master's course on writing for children and teens at Goldsmiths, University of London, at least once a term, a student would bring in a story with a young main character, but the writer didn't realise that it wasn't a book for children/teens. It takes more than a young protagonist to make a children's book. The following four-part test will help you determine whether what you are writing is, in fact, a book for children/teens/young adults.

Test 1: Is your protagonist the same age or older than your intended readership?

Children and teens tend to read aspirationally. Protagonists are often a few years older than the readership. Teens probably won't read a book starring a 10 year-old, for example. Nor will publishers acquire a book for readers 5 to 8 years old that features a 15 year-old main character.

Test 2: Is your narrative child-centric?
Make sure your young protagonist is leading the story and it's a story about and for children. Or is your young character observing and recounting a story with adult characters and adult problems at its heart? One quick check is to look at how many adult characters you have in your story. In my opinion, your young characters should outnumber the adults.

Your story must concentrate on issues and ideas important to children. It's not that you can't have adult issues in the story – a real estate development or parents' money problems, for example – but the story must focus on how these problems will affect children. The new housing project might displace a favourite playground; parents' money woes might mean your teen can't attend their prom or take part in a school trip.

It's vital that your child/teen main character solve the issue or problem. She/he/they must take action. Conflict can happen to your main character, but she/he/they must do more than simply react. They must drive the action. And a parent, teacher or guardian can't step in and solve the problem. Your character at some point in your story must take control.

Test 3: Is your word count appropriate for your readership?

The table below shows some ballpark figures. There are great books that are shorter and longer than the parameters I list, but it's helpful to have a range to consider. Every other year for eighteen years, I've organized an anthology and we ask writers to select the appropriate age range for their story. They get this wrong quite often: we might see a YA novel that's only 10,000 words or a 15,000-word book for 5 year-olds.

There is a move for more High Low (Hi-Lo) books – high concept, low vocabulary/readability level – for children and teens to help boost the declining number of young people who read for pleasure. If you are writing one of these, your word counts may be lower.

Word count

Type of book	Age of reader	Typical word count
Early/first reader/chapter books (illustrated but not picture books)	5 year-olds	Not longer than 3,000 words
Story books	5–7 year-olds	Up to 8,000 words
Young fiction	7–9 year-olds	Up to 15,000 words
Middle-grade fiction	9–12 year-olds	35,000 to 45,000 words
Young adult fiction	13 years and older	60,000 to 85,000 words

Does your word count match your intended reader? If not, why not? Cut or expand your story appropriately.

Test 4: Is your story written from the perspective of a child experiencing the action or an adult looking back with the benefit of hindsight?

Harper Lee's classic, *To Kill a Mockingbird*, features a young protagonist, Scout. Yet it's definitely not a children's book. An adult Scout is recounting the experience of one summer when she was young. In the story, Scout ages from 5 to 8 years old, but the story is clearly for young adult to adult readers.

If you've discovered that what you are writing is not for children/teens – and that is your intention – or perhaps you've misjudged the age range, stop your revision process and address this.

Checklist

☐ **Does your story achieve what you hoped it would?**

If not, can you identify why not? Note areas of concern on your manuscript and start a list of revision ideas. Working through the exercises in this book should help you tackle these issues.

☐ **Is it important to you?**

Are you obsessed with your idea? Thinking about it day and night? If your book is published you will be living with it for months, years, the rest of your life. Do you know why you are writing it? Why are you the only one who can tell this story? What has kept you interested in this idea? You must love your story. Like any romance, you may fall in and out of love at points, but overall you should have a deep affection for your story.

☐ **Is it a story?**

Remember that your story must have the following three elements:

Concept + Character x Conflict = Novel

See Chapters 2 and 3 for help with any issues you might have with character and plot respectively.

☐ **Is it compelling and unique?**

Make sure you can highlight what makes your story unique. If it's a witch story, how does it differ from the hundreds of other witch stories in print?

☐ **Are you satisfied with your pitch?**

Did writing it flag any issues with your story? If so, can you write a pitch that reflects the book you want to write? Make notes on how you might revise your book to reflect this new pitch. Keep honing your pitch until you are satisfied that it will entice agents to read beyond your query letter. (More on agents and next steps in Chapter 12.) When you've finished your revision – if your book has changed significantly – you may want to rewrite the pitch.

Is it a book for children/teens/young adults?

It's fine if you realised that your book is for adult readers – as long as that's what you want to do. If your intention is to write a book for children or teens, then cut or adjust your work to make the book *for* children, not *about* them. Centre the story on your young protagonist, and revise accordingly. The chapters on plot and character will help focus your story for young readers.

Now that you've tested your idea, it's time for the real work to begin. We are going to break down your novel, build it back up, and make it the best book it can possibly be!

CHAPTER 2

Character by character

Our spotlight now shifts to the protagonists of your story. If readers don't care about your main character, they won't read on. The characters you've created feel real to you – maybe they even speak to you as you write – but has your vision for each character been translated onto the page?

Your story demands a unique cast of three-dimensional characters. Your protagonist must change and grow throughout the story. In *Story Genius: How to use brain science to go beyond outlining and write a riveting novel*, Lisa Cron succinctly defines the ideal journey of a main character:

> All stories revolve around how someone solves a single, escalating problem they can't avoid ... one that causes the protagonist to struggle with a specific internal conflict at every turn, so that at the end she sees things quite differently than she did at the beginning.

This chapter tests if your characters live up to this challenge.

We will isolate important characters and ensure each is authentic. We will review their presence in the story and their place in your cast of characters. Some characters will get makeovers; others might be combined or eliminated. The result will be characters who will propel readers to the final full stop.

Highlighting each character

Open your manuscript on your computer and save it as a new document. (I always keep an original, untouched version of my manuscript. Throughout this book, I'll encourage you to experiment with your draft and discard what's not working. By having an original draft, you can feel more comfortable working through the exercises that follow.)

In this new file, I want you to give each character name a unique colour. Microsoft Word (like most word-processing software) has a *Find* and *Replace* function. In Word, it's under the *Home* tab on the right of the header ribbon. A dialogue box will appear when you click the *Replace* option.

Type in one character's name in the *Find what*: box then copy and paste the same name in the *Replace with*: box. It's important that the name in both boxes is exactly the same – no extra spaces at the end or different capitalization. Next hit the *Format* button at the bottom-left corner of the box and select *Highlight*. (You may need to hit the *More* button if you don't see the *Format* button.) Choose one of the 15 colour options that appear when you select the *Text Highlight Colour* button. Now click *Replace All*. Do this for each important character.

A dialogue box will come up with the number of times the name appears in your manuscript. Make a note of this number. When you've done this for every character, review the total number of mentions of each character. Is it what you expected?

If you are writing in the first person, highlighting your protagonist's name won't find every reference. (Highlighting 'I' doesn't work too well.) This won't be a problem because, in a first-person story, your protagonist will be in every scene.

Your manuscript should now have its cast of characters in a rainbow-assortment of colours. I like to print this new document. You'll be surprised at how the simple act of reading your manuscript on a printed page will flag issues and errors you've overlooked in the many, many times you've read your story on the computer. Also, the act of editing by hand will give you two opportunities to review any corrections – one when you pencil it in and another when you type it into the document.

Exercise

Reading for each character

1. Aerial view

The first thing I do with my colour-coded draft is spread the pages out in order on the floor. Step back and look at where your rainbow of characters appear in your story. Are there characters that should have a greater presence? When I did this exercise for an early draft of *Dark Parties*, my protagonist's love interest Braydon appeared in Chapter 1, but I was surprised to find that his name wasn't even mentioned again until Chapter 7. If I wanted the reader to care about my love triangle, this simply wouldn't do. I added another scene with Braydon that enhanced my romantic subplot and also had my main character think of him from time to time – as teenagers certainly do with their crushes.

Scan your story. Are there characters that always appear together? Maybe there's a group of friends. Is each friend necessary, or could you combine two of your characters to simplify your cast? Are there characters that pop up only sporadically? This may be okay, but ask yourself if they are essential. If not, sharpen your pencil and strike the character from the story!

2. Protagonist(s)

You want to spend the most time studying your main character. Remember what we discussed in the previous chapter from *Revision and Self-Editing for Publication* by James Scott Bell: unforgettable characters have 'Grit, wit and it'. Is your protagonist unique, authentic and – to echo Blake Snyder in *Save the Cat! Strikes Back* – 'on the verge of change'?

Often protagonists are too passive. They narrate the story. They observe. Things happen *to* them. They are batted around like a ball in the pinball plot machine. Your main character should be one of the most interesting characters in the book – if not *the* most interesting. Does your main character command the spotlight?

Answer the following questions about your main character.

1. What does your main character want?

2. Why does she/he/they want it?

3. What happens if she/he/they doesn't get it?

4. Why should I care if she/he/they gets it?

5. Why is this crisis happening now?

6. Why can't your character just walk away? Why does she/he/they have to soldier on?

Your answers to these questions determine what's driving the story and what's at stake for your protagonist. If these were difficult to answer or your responses are a bit wishy-washy, stop and determine how to strengthen your character. As you read your manuscript – focusing only on your main character – you can start to make adjustments to add weight to your character's journey.

Exercise

The lives of your protagonist

Many years ago, when I took a class titled *Murder in America*, the professor invited an FBI profiler to speak. He said to solve a crime, he needed to uncover the lives of the victim – *lives*, plural. He said we all have a public, a private and a secret life. Our public life is what anyone could know about us. I'm a writer who lives in London. I'm married. I've written several books for children and teens. Our private life is known only to a close few. These are the secrets, fears and personal details we share with friends and family. I met my husband while in a queue at Universal Studio, for example. And finally, the profiler said we all have a secret life: the things we keep to ourselves and never, ever tell a living soul. You know what I'm talking about. No examples from me!

When evaluating your main character, ask:

What is their public life?

What is their private life? Who are the people they confide in?

What is their secret life?

This is an easy way to deepen your character by adding layers to their personality. How can your responses add depth to your character? How will you show this to your readers?

Exercise

Profound and surface journeys

Noah Lukeman's book *The Plot Thickens* forever changed the way I create characters. He explained that great protagonists must have both a surface journey: to solve a crime, to survive, to find love, etc., and a profound journey: an inner journey of self-realization. The profound journey is your main character's emotional arc.

The surface journey is the easy one! It's the action of the story. The profound journey is a bit trickier. How will your main character change and grow and how will the surface journey help them evolve? The two must be linked. If you're working on a romance, the surface journey will be focused on getting the guy or the girl. Your character's profound journey will be one of the things keeping them apart. Are they selfish and need to learn to be selfless, for example?

In Candy Gourlay's beautiful book *Wild Song*, her main character Luki, a teen girl from a tribe in the mountains of the Philippines, travels to the United States and is put on display at the 1904 World's Fair. Luki's surface journey is a quest, but it's also a profound journey to understand herself and her place in the world. In my middle grade series *Chasing Danger*, the surface journey of my main character, Chase, is to survive and catch the villains. She's on an exotic island in the Maldives when modern-day pirates attack. Lots of exciting action ensues, but there's more to Chase's story. She also discovers that her mother is in prison. While she's saving the day, she struggles with questions of identity – is she 'bad' like her mother? In both of these stories, the characters' surface journeys influence their profound dilemmas.

Reviewing or discovering the journeys of your characters will dramatically improve your story.

What is your protagonist's surface journey?

What is her/his/their profound journey?

How are the two connected?

If you are struggling with identifying your character's profound journey, this may signal a two-dimensional character. Now's the time to stop and enhance the emotional journey of your character.

Interrogating your protagonist

You can do the next two exercises as you read your novel again with a spotlight on how your main character, who is so alive in your head, has translated on the page. You may have written a backstory or filled out questionnaires before you started writing. What I want you to note in the next exercises are the details that you include in this draft.

Exercise

Protagonist profile

This exercise will help ensure that your main character feels real. Readers crave three-dimensional characters that are believable. Creating a character profile for your protagonist can test whether you know enough about your main character and if these glorious subtleties appear on the page. Your profile could include the following topics, but you may have other character details you'd like to track, depending on your story.

Name: Include full name and any nicknames

Age:

Personality: I try to boil down the essence of a character – a sort of shortcut. It might help to think of her/his/their public, private and secret lives here.

Journeys:

- Profound
- Surface

Writing style/voice: I study the voice and try to develop prompts for the writing style. I might write in this section something like: poetic descriptions, quirky observations, negative self-talk, sentence fragments. More on this in Chapter 6 about voice.

Appearance: You might include height, weight, hair, style of dress, etc.

Defining feature: If someone was trying to point out your character in a crowd, what one feature would they mention? He's the one with the pink hair or glasses with black rectangular frames. It could be a scar, hairstyle, piece of jewellery or clothing they always wear or a tattoo.

History/backstory: You may have already created documents with character questionnaires or histories. Note what you include in your story, any anecdotes or flashbacks, for example.

Details: Maybe they have a bouncy stride, a favourite colour or are a film buff. Note anything that you include in your manuscript. This will help with character consistency if you need to revise your manuscript again.

Miscellaneous: It's also good to have a catch-all for anything that's important to remember but doesn't fit neatly in the categories above.

If any of these areas are blank, spend time developing the character a bit more and add these changes to your story.

Exercise

Trace your protagonist's emotional journey

Readers are drawn to nuanced and complex characters, characters on the verge of change, characters that will, in some way, be unrecognizable by the end of the work. In *The Plot Thickens*, Lukeman calls these characters *ripe characters*. This doesn't mean your characters are uninteresting at the start. You need to give us enough to make us want to follow them from the opening page. What is their unique way of looking at the world? A great example is Katniss from *The Hunger Games*. She's not the most likable character in the opening pages. We are told even the cat hates – or at least distrusts – Katniss. But soon we discover intriguing details; she's a skilled archer, for example. By the end of Chapter 1, she's stepped in to save her younger sister. That's a protagonist we can cheer for!

As you read with a focus on your protagonist, highlight – literally, with a coloured highlighter – the emotional journey of your main character. Highlight the moments when you reveal something about the main character's emotional state. When you are finished, read only the lines you've highlighted. Is the character's emotional journey clear? Does it evolve? Can we see why your character is changing and growing? Eureka moments aren't as interesting as gradual change. Show us those epiphanies on the page so we can learn alongside your characters.

In an early draft of *Dark Parties*, I realised my main character Neva had an emotional journey that flip-flopped enough times to cause whiplash. Yes, human beings can repeatedly change their minds and go back and forth when trying to solve an important problem. Our characters will too, but try to smooth your character's emotional journey. If possible, show us a gradual shift in how the character's surface journey ultimately leads to a realization in her/his/their profound journey.

**Stop and read your book
focusing on your protagonist.**

Secondary character examination

Once you've finessed your protagonist so she/he/they sparks on the page, let's give some love to each significant secondary character. Read your story character by character, using the colour-coded manuscript you created earlier in the chapter. Reading just one character's scenes in succession will help you hone her/his/their emotional journey as well as check for consistency throughout the novel. Isolating and engaging with one character at a time can help you create a more dynamic and three-dimensional cast.

Character analysis

Each time you read for a new character, consider the following:

- **What is each character's role in the story?** Write it down. Make each character fight for her/his/their life.

- **Is each character necessary?** If you can eliminate a character with minimal effect to your overall story, do it.

- **Is each character compelling and distinct?** Not simply that they look and sound unique, but consider smaller details. Are their names different from each other so readers won't get confused? Certainly no Oliver and Olivia; perhaps not even characters with the same first initial, so no Sam and Susan.

This is when you might add a few lines here and there to enhance any flat characters. Maybe adjust their world view, their history, experiences, talents, skills or quirks. It's amazing how adding a few strategic lines throughout can bring a secondary character to life.

- **Does the character's dialogue have an original voice?** After I've read through the book, focusing on one specific character, I will read aloud each line of dialogue attributed to that character. That's it. One line of dialogue after another and give each character a unique way of speaking. My goal is to be able to identify who said the line based on content, tone and language – even if the piece of dialogue isn't attributed.

Exercise

Secondary character profiles

As you review each character, create a profile, similar to the one you created for your protagonist. I usually create a new document titled *Cast List*. Then create separate sections for each character. Customize the sections you include in your profiles. There may be other traits or information you want to track for each character.

Name:

Age:

Personality: Similar to what you did for your protagonist, write down a few lines that define each character. How are they special and unique? If you have a comic sidekick character, make sure you add additional traits to keep them from being clichéd. Maybe your comic sidekick is deeply self-critical and fiercely vegan.

Voice: For secondary characters you might note their particular way of speaking. For example, do they have a catchphrase or a phrase they overuse? Any dialect or linguistic ticks?

Appearance: Make sure you've consistently described your characters. I've had characters with green eyes in the first chapter which I've accidentally changed to blue in a later chapter. If they are short of stature, do they consistently see the world from their correct height? Do you tend to lead with a particular trait, hair colour, for example? (Don't laugh! This was something I used to do.)

Defining feature:

History/backstory:

Details: Note any details that you include in your manuscript.

Miscellaneous:

If any of these areas are blank for a character, give that character a bit more attention and revise your story accordingly. These character profiles will help keep your characters consistent throughout the book and on any future drafts.

- **Scrutinize each detail.** Is it appropriate for the character's age and experience? Unless you are writing a character who is the same age, gender and race with a similar background as yourself, make sure you haven't leaked onto the page. This can happen sometimes when adults are writing child characters. Make sure your young characters aren't wise beyond their years or make references that aren't appropriate.

- **Set up and pay off.** Don't leave any loose ends for readers. If you spotlight key details and information – maybe your character has a fear of blue bubble gum or collects buttons – those are good, quirky details. Will we discover why she/he/they have gum phobia and adore buttons? These details must be important to the story. If not, why are you asking your reader to remember this detail? The same with secrets: how will they serve your story?

**Stop and tweak each character
based on what you've discovered.**

Character continuum

Organize your cast of characters on a variety of continuums. How will they complement and confound each other? Build your cast to create opportunities and conflicts. Also watch out for stereotypical or typecast characters. No person is fully good or evil, so make sure all of your significant characters are well rounded. The continuums you use will be based on the type of book you are writing. A few ideas are:

Brains	to	Brawn
Optimist	to	Pessimist
Good	to	Evil
Funny	to	Serious

Plot each character on these continuums. The more variety in your plotting, the more opportunities you create for engaging interactions among your characters.

In *Chasing Danger*, I generate conflict and humour because one character *acts first* and another *thinks first*. This complementary behaviour is how they survive the many disasters I hurl at them.

If you find that you have characters that are too similar, consider how to make your cast less homogenous. Are your characters appropriately culturally and physically diverse for the story you want to tell? We'll cover issues of cultural authenticity in Chapter 7. Maybe diversifying your cast of characters will introduce a more interesting perspective.

Tangled characters

Create a character–relationship diagram. Plot your significant characters based on their connection to the main character and other characters. The more tangled the characters, the better. If you find characters with only one connection, you might want to determine whether they are really necessary to the novel or find ways to enhance their relationships with other characters.

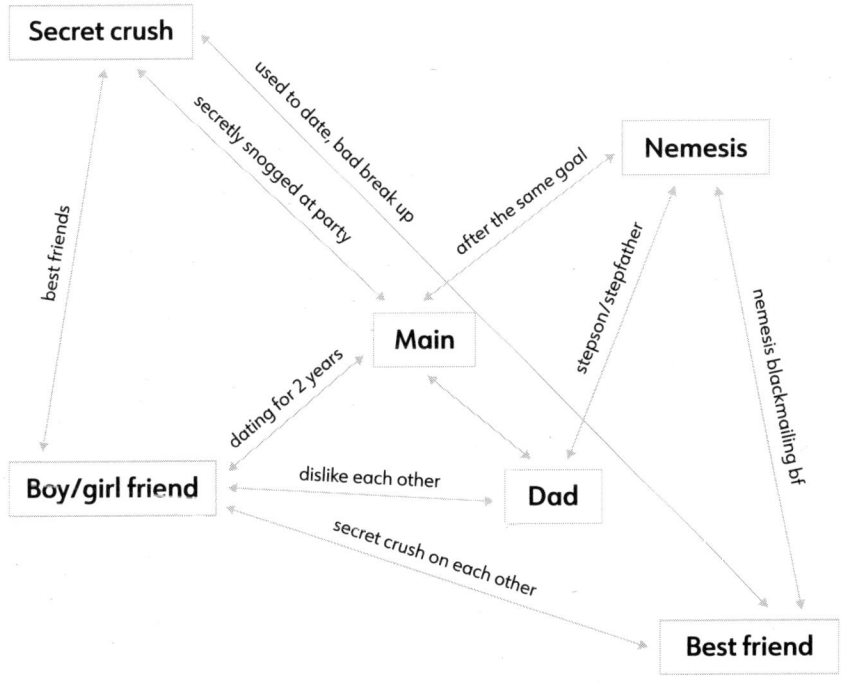

Exercise

Introducing your protagonist

Review the first 1,000 words of your story. Make a list of what you **show** and **tell** about your protagonist.

1. ....

2. ....

3. ....

4. ....

5. ....

6. ....

7. ....

8. ....

9. ....

10. ....

In *Millions*, Frank Cottrell-Boyce so cleverly and concisely paints the two main characters, who are brothers, from the opening lines: 'If our Anthony was telling this story, he'd start with the money.' Later in the paragraph we learn about our narrator who is Anthony's brother: 'Personally I like to start with the patron saint of whatever it is.'

EXERCISE IN ACTION

I used this exercise on one of my many works-in-progress. The following is the first 400 words of a young adult novel titled *Mind Fields*. Below the extract, I note what I show and tell readers about my main character.

I'm in the middle of my pre-pageant ritual when it happens again. I pump up the volume on the radio and dance around my bedroom in my lucky lavender bra and panties, trying to disappear into the music.

Please, not now.

The song stops abruptly, and a fuzzy feeling buzzes at the edge of my sanity. The radio announcer's voice blares, "Mortonsville, make a difference. Join Indiana-native Scott Anwir as he kicks off his senatorial election campaign at a rally in the town square tonight … "

I reach to switch off the radio, but another voice comes on, and he's all 'Unite America' blah, blah, blah. I don't get all that boring political stuff. I should try. I've just turned 18 and can vote. But what does some dumb senate race in Indiana matter anyway? I flick off the radio, but the guy's voice lingers in my brain.

And that's when the weird-yet-familiar feeling takes hold. I grab for the bookcase to steady myself. My fingers find a heart-shaped tiara. I lock eyes with the girl in my full-length mirror. The girl is me – Tyra Giselle Bottoms – but for a moment, I don't recognize her. Curls cascade down her back, a combination of hair extensions and extra light ash 182 with a splash of auburn 36. Her eyes are framed with glitter-tipped lashes. Her complexion shines a flawless faux tan with an unnatural orange hue. Her teeth have been straightened, capped and bleached to neon white. Her acrylic nails shine with Cha Ching Cherry.

It's like I'm seeing myself for the first time; the image in my brain doesn't match the *Top Model* Frankenstein staring back at me. I fling the tiara at that girl to make her disappear. The mirror cracks with a pop. Hundreds of lines shoot from the black dot where the tiara made contact. The mirror fractures into a spider web of distorted me's. I feel myself splitting into a hundred pieces.

These episodes where I'm me and not me usually last a few seconds, but not this time.

My vision softens and blurs. I have that elevator sensation as if I'm being lifted from the basement to the penthouse with a whoosh …

Images flicker before my eyes – a slideshow in funhouse fast forward. These aren't memories. This isn't a dream. It's not like watching myself in the thousand-and-one beauty pageant videos Mom has made of me. I don't see myself. I'm experiencing – living – each scene.

---

1. This character is an experienced beauty pageant contestant. We are told this is her *pre-pageant* ritual. She has a tiara on her bookcase. Her mom has taken a *thousand-and-one beauty pageant videos* of her.

2. She's body confident, dancing around her room in bra and panties.

3. She's experiencing anxiety or a mental health issue. We are told she's *trying* to disappear into the music, and she thinks *Please, not now.* Also she's experiencing a fuzzy feeling, staggering around her room and breaks a mirror. She doesn't recognize herself. She tells us that she's had these *episodes* before.

4. She lives in Mortonsville, Indiana.

5. She's 18 years old.

6. She doesn't care about politics.

7. Her name is Tyra Giselle Bottoms.

8. She has hair-extension-enhanced long, curly dyed blonde hair. Her teeth are straightened, capped and bleached. She's wearing glitter-tipped lashes and has a fake tan, and her acrylic nails are painted Cha Ching Cherry.

What is the balance of showing and telling in your piece? Don't tell us too much. Let the details of your character evolve from the action. Sprinkle in conservatively any details you offer. The opening pages are not the place for backstory or dumps of information: neither will compel readers to read on, nor make them adore your character.

Checklist

☐ **Does your protagonist feel three-dimensional with an original voice and an emotional journey that compels the reader from the first to the last page?**

If you are still worried that your main character isn't compelling enough, stop and take the time to really unlock her/his/their profound and surface journeys as well as their public, private and secret lives. You may want to do some work off the page, maybe filling out one or more of the character questionnaires you can find online. Determine how you will enhance your main character. You might need to add scenes to demonstrate the new features you've discovered. Don't move on until you are happy that your main character springs to life on the page and is truly the star of the story.

☐ **Is each character necessary, connected and unique?**

I hope the character analysis, diagram and continuums helped you hone your cast of characters. This is the time to cut characters that aren't pulling their weight. Also by reading your novel character by character, you've identified and fixed any inconsistencies as well as enhanced each character so that each feels authentic and essential to the story.

CHAPTER 3

Finding the plot

Let's focus on plot now. What story are you trying to tell and are you successful? This is the time to fine-tune your main plot and subplots. I've included several exercises that will help you uncover and enhance key themes and shape the reader's experience.

Structural edit

Many writers revise their novel as they go, but until you have a draft, you can't fully appreciate what your story is about and how the drama should unfold. Do not start polishing until you have solved overall issues of plot, subplot, character arcs, pacing and narration. Sometimes we line-edit to avoid the big issues, but the structural edit should always come first! Don't waste time refining specific sentences when you might ditch an entire chapter. Only after you are happy with the overall shape of your story should you dig deeper and finesse the words on the page.

Car parks

Cutting big sections of writing is never fun – especially if you've edited your draft – and then, oh, you edited it a bit more. But you must be brave. When I start my revision, I create a new document that I title *[Novel Name] Parking Lot* (and Brits might name *Car Park*). Every time I realise that a paragraph or more will need to be removed, I copy and paste it in my Parking Lot. It makes me feel better that those words aren't erased forever. On occasion I discover that I was wrong and reinstate the section. Other times I find another way to use it in the novel. If I'm cutting characters or subplots, they can sometimes spark another story.

What is plot?

In her book *Writing Fiction: A Guide to Narrative Craft*, Janet Burroway gives a clear definition of story and plot:

> A *story* is a series of events recorded in their chronological order. A *plot* is a series of events deliberately arranged so as to reveal their dramatic, thematic and emotional significance.

The exercises in this chapter will help you shape your plot to maximize the drama, theme and emotional signature of your story.

Plotting for young readers

Plot plays an even greater role for young readers. Before we dive into your plot, here are a few guidelines for books for young readers.

1. Engage readers from the opening page.

Adults allow an author at least a bit of indulgence. They might hang in there with a book for fifty pages before it truly grips them. Most young readers won't wait. You must hook them from the first page so don't ramp up to your story; kickstart it as soon as possible and keep it moving swiftly.

As I mentioned earlier, for many years, I organized an anthology for unpublished and unagented children's writers. Each time, I read the first 4,000 words of more than 200 stories to pick the top twelve to include in the anthology. Many submissions were rejected because authors sent a preamble. In those cases, the first 4,000 words may have set the stage, but the story never really took off.

The younger your reader, the quicker you should get to the inciting incident – that moment that sets your story in motion and changes your main character's life forever. One of my favourite young adult books is David Levithan's *Every Day*. On the first page the chapter is titled 'Day 5994', so we know the story is already in progress. He tells us immediately that the main character wakes up in a different body each day, and it's always been like that. Jennifer Killick's *Dread Wood*, the seriously scary adventures of four Year 7s serving detention on a Saturday, starts with a blood-curdling scream at the end of Chapter 1. In Tọlá Okogwu's *Onyeka and the Academy of the Sun*, Onyeka first experiences her superpower when her wild and wonderful hair somehow saves her best friend from drowning at the end of Chapter 2. In all of these books I'm quickly hooked and eager to discover what happens next.

2. Ensure your plot is child-centric and age-appropriate.

We touched on this in the chapter on interrogating your idea. Make sure that not only are your plot/subplots appropriate for the age of your reader, but also that the action is driven by your young main character. For example, relationship issues can be the plot or subplot for almost any age, but romance that ends in anything more than a kiss should be reserved for young adult stories. Middle-grade romances tend to be centred on a crush and end with a kiss. Books for younger readers typically don't have a romantic plot at all, unless it's one dealing with a parent's relationship.

3. Create plots and subplots with the appropriate complexity for your reader.

These are not rigid rules, but it's helpful to have some guidelines. There are published books that have more or fewer plots than I'm suggesting. But if your novel doesn't conform to the following, consider if you are asking too much – or too little – of your reader.

Target age of reader	Suggested number of plots and subplots
5–8 years	One plot, usually no subplots. Books for this age group are almost exclusively series fiction. Often there won't be much character development. The main character is the same throughout the series.
7–9 years	A main plot and a subplot with a character arc. The main character will learn something important and be changed by the end of the book.
9–12 years Middle grade	A main plot and a few subplots and an emotional journey for the main character.

| 13+ years
Young adult | A main plot with several subplots, one of which is usually a romance, and a significant and thoughtful emotional journey for the protagonist. |

4. Maintain the momentum until the end.

Don't give your readers the chance to look away. I'm not saying you should 'dumb down' anything. I'm also not saying that you shouldn't have moments – not chapters or scenes, but moments – where you let your story breathe. But you must keep things moving to keep readers engaged – especially now, with readers so accustomed to the brevity of TikTok and YouTube.

A quick analysis

It's time for a pop quiz about your plot! Respond quickly to the next seven questions, which were inspired by a questionnaire that was shared with me regarding how the BBC reviews a script. If you have to think too much or aren't sure about the answer to a specific question, leave it blank – for now. This is a diagnostic tool to identify plot problems. Give yourself half an hour. On the following pages, I'll examine each question and offer suggestions on how to deal with any issues you uncover. In some cases, I'll also point you to the appropriate chapter in the book that can help.

1. Can you identify your main plot and subplots?

Your main plot drives the story. Your subplots – sometimes called secondary plots – feed into the main plot but are not the main problem/issue/conflict of the story.

Tracey Mathias' *Silence is Also A Lie* is a great example of how the main plots and subplots are interwoven. Her main plot is a love story between Zara and Ash, whose romance is confounded because of a mystery subplot. Ash's sister Sophie died and only Zara knows how. The other significant subplots stem from the setting. The story is set in an alternate version of Britain – one where anyone born outside the country (labelled as an illegal) is arrested and deported. Zara is an 'illegal'.

Now it's your turn!

Main Plot

Subplots

1.

2.

3.

4.

2. What is the event that sets the story in motion?

3. What are the emotional and/or physical obstacles that confront the main character?

4. What is at stake? What will happen if the main character doesn't get what she/he/they wants?

5. Why should we care?

6. How does it end? Does the main character get what she/he/they wants?

7. Is it satisfying?

Solutions to your plot problems

Now we consider your answers to each question and what it might mean for your revision.

1. Can you identify your main plot and subplots?

MAIN PLOT

I hope this was an easy one. If not, considering the genre of your book can help. If you are writing a romance, then it's about winning the object of your main character's affection. If you are writing a mystery, it's about figuring out whodunnit. Quests can focus on finding an important object or person. And disaster stories are about surviving.

Maybe you found that you have two or more plots vying for the primary position. Often if you are writing young adult fiction, a romance will play a significant role in your story. For middle grade, it can be a relationship – often friendship – that intertwines with the main plot. It's important to determine which plot is the main plot. Stories that try to serve two plots equally can feel chaotic and confusing. Are you writing a mystery with a romance or a romance that has a mystery? It may seem like splitting hairs, but your story will benefit from having one plot – and only one – that drives the story.

SUBPLOTS

If you are writing for readers seven years and older, your book should have at least one subplot. But how many is too many? The next chapter offers a few different exercises to discover and wrangle your subplots.

2. What is the event that sets the story in motion?

This is called the inciting incident. It's the moment that causes the chain reaction that will change the main character's life forever. Sometimes it's difficult to pinpoint. The inciting incident in the *Harry Potter* series is the arrival of Harry's invitation to Hogwarts. You could argue that his destiny was sealed when he received the lightning scar on his head as a baby, or even further back than that when his parents met. But the moment that sets the story in motion is a literal invitation. Dave Cousins' *Fifteen Days Without a Head* begins when 15-year-old Laurence's mum goes missing. A terrorist attack changes Aaliyah's life forever in A.M. Dassu's *Fight Back*. Dav Pilkey kicks off his best-selling series with George and Harold hypnotizing Principal Krupp so he believes he's the hero of the boys' homemade comic – *Captain Underpants*.

The inciting incident usually happens on the page. There might be good reasons to report that the inciting incident has happened, but generally your readers should experience it alongside your protagonist.

What moment in your story moves your character to action? As I indicated before, the younger your target reader, the sooner your inciting incident should happen.

3. What are the emotional and/or physical obstacles that confront the main character?

When I give creative writing talks at schools, I say that authors are horrible people. Sara Grant, the person, tries to be the nicest person she possibly can be. (Okay, I don't always succeed, but I try!) But author Sara Grant creates characters she loves and then gives them the worst days of their lives. Don't make it easy for your characters to get what they want. Now is the time to decide if you have too few or too many obstacles.

Obstacles can be physical: a natural disaster or the many miles between your character and her true love. But they can also be emotional or philosophical: the character's true love is dating another person, or your character lacks confidence. Character flaws can be the obstacle. Think of Scrooge, for example. He's greedy, cruel and narcissistic. Through the course of *A Christmas Carol* he overcomes those flaws, learning charity and humanity – and that alters his future. If you are writing for readers over seven years old, you will want to consider the emotional arc of your main character. I hope you've already addressed your character issues in the previous chapter.

Look at the list of obstacles you've erected for your main character. Are they too similar? I get frustrated when the main character repeats the same mistakes again and again. You can have a character make an oafish comment once or twice, for example, to show this flaw, but if it happens too often, your character may become less sympathetic.

In the next chapter we will dissect the action in your book. If you're concerned that you have too many or too few obstacles, this will be your chance to correct that.

4. What is at stake? What will happen if the main character doesn't get what she/he/they wants?

The stakes must be high. Mysteries, quests and action-adventure stories often feature literal life-or-death struggles. And though a teen not being asked to the school dance isn't life-or-death, it can certainly feel that way to the person involved.

When the going gets tough, why doesn't your character just walk away? The answer must be because they can't. James Scott Bell calls this the *adhesive*. Why is your character stuck with seeing the struggle through to the bitter end?

Make sure the stakes are high enough. If your reader isn't invested in your character's success, they will stop reading. Raise the stakes enough to make sure your story doesn't sag in the middle, and that its dramatic pull stays constant.

5. Why should we care?

When I've asked this question at workshops, writers are often stumped. Your character obviously must care deeply about achieving the story's goal – and you must make your readers care deeply too. If you don't have a good answer to this question, turn to a book you loved for help. Why did you care? How did the author do it? Typically, the answer lies with the character. It might be that you haven't created a truly three-dimensional character. It could be that the stakes aren't high enough. Re-visit the previous chapter for any character-related issues. The next chapter will help you with pace, tension and drama.

6. How does it end? Does the main character get what she/he/they wants?

In the opening pages, you make a promise to your readers: this is the journey you will take them on. Your ending should keep that promise. And the climax must happen *on the page* – never be reported to the reader.

Most books for children or young adults will have a happy ending. The main character will achieve the goal. We are giving our young readers a safe space to explore difficult issues and circumstances. At the very least, endings for young readers should be hopeful.

7. Is it satisfying?

You might not be the best person to respond to this question. Obviously, *you* think the ending works because you wrote it! However, sometimes I've found that writers are so fatigued by the end of the first draft that they rush the ending. Or they write *an* ending while knowing in their heart of hearts that they haven't written *the* ending. If your gut is telling you your ending isn't working, listen. Good enough is never okay when it comes to the ending – or indeed really any aspect of your novel, but especially the finale. (If you think your ending is problematic, Chapter 10 will help you sort it out.)

Tackling your theme

Some writers start with a theme or issue they want to tackle. They develop their stories with this at the very heart. Some unearth the theme retrospectively. They write a draft and let themes bubble up. They only spot their theme once the story is finished. Or maybe theme isn't something you've considered yet. That's fine too. Now's your chance to analyse and enhance your theme – whether it's something you consider proactively or reactively.

I've had a few opportunities over the years to read submissions packs for publishers, agents and competitions. Nothing struck fear into my heart like a synopsis or a cover letter that boasted the theme of the book: teach children the importance of recycling, stop bullying, show the power of positive thinking, save the whales, etc. My concern – before I even read the opening line – was that the theme would be delivered like a sledgehammer to my frontal lobe.

When it comes to including a theme in fiction, don't teach your readers a lesson, but give them an amazing story that opens the door for discussion. Show, don't tell. It's advice that writers hear over and over and over. It usually refers to summarizing the action rather than letting readers experience the drama. But it's also good advice when considering the theme or message of a novel. Let the theme evolve from the action.

The books that I love, books that stay with me long after I've finished them, not only have a fascinating story, but also open a dialogue with the reader. They show an issue's multiple, beautiful shades of grey. I appreciate a story that highlights an issue's complexity without offering an easy answer – because in life, one rarely exists. I write with an issue/theme in mind, not a moral.

At a British Society of Children's Book Writers and Illustrators (SCBWI) conference, award-winning children's author Marcus Sedgwick once commented that, in writing an entire novel, he allowed himself one line that expressed his theme. This type of restraint – not preaching to your readers – keeps the theme from overshadowing the story. This economy of message respects the reader. The word diversity appears only once in *Dark Parties* – even though it's at the heart of my reasons for writing it.

Exercise

Shaping your theme

Did you write your story with a theme in mind? If so, write it down.

If not, that doesn't mean you aren't sharing a message with your readers. One way to check is consider what Robert McKee in *Story* calls the controlling idea – the story's ultimate meaning expressed through the action and emotion of the book's climax. What is your book trying to say? Good conquers evil? You find love when you accept yourself?

What do you want your readers to take away from your story?

A few examples:

For *Dark Parties*, my controlling idea was: a society will fail when individuality is destroyed. For *Half Lives*, it was: civilizations survive because of one person's sacrifice.

Is your controlling idea what you thought it was? When I did this exercise for *Dark Parties*, a book with female empowerment at its heart, I realized that I had a boy swooping in to rescue my female protagonist. What? No! I had to minimize the swoop factor and make sure my strong, fierce protagonist saved herself. Make sure that where you leave your readers – that is, the message they take away – is what you intended.

Scan your story and highlight any passages that illuminate your theme. You might have a moment when, in dialogue, a character shares the theme. Or you might find that one line that expresses your theme. Also highlight moments where your theme is in action. Find how you've sprinkled your theme like Hansel and Gretel's breadcrumbs throughout your story.

Review and reflect on the passages you've highlighted. Is your theme seeded throughout? Do these moments build on each other? Eureka epiphanies – those revelations that come out of nowhere

– usually are not as powerful as those that are planned and spring from the action of your book. Take the time you need to smooth your theme in your story. You might need to add scenes or moments that will help bring your theme to life.

If your theme is something like: putting others first enriches our own life. Maybe your protagonist is selfish and must learn to be selfless to achieve their goal. In an early scene we need to see how her/his/their selfish behaviour is detrimental. We might need to see a selfless act from someone else. We could also have the protagonist try and fail to put another person first before ultimately performing a selfless act that saves the day. If there's a story that moved you, do this same exercise for that book. See how that author weaved her/his/their magic, and try to do something similar for your readers.

Stop and review how theme is threaded throughout your book and make any needed adjustments.

Managing the middle

Middles can be murder. You've set the story in motion, but how do you maintain the appropriate amount of tension/suspense/surprise/drama to keep readers reading?

Exercise

Plot like Fireman Sam

I attended a workshop years ago run by Cornerstones Literary Consultancy where writer, producer and showrunner Jen Upton was one of the presenters. She has worked on several children's TV programmes, including the cartoon *Fireman Sam*, the classic British children's show. She passed along a trusted plotting strategy from her television work, which is the best and quickest plot test I've ever known.

She said that, when working on an episode, they'd evaluate it with this simple three-point plot test. It's basically checking to see that you're building tension throughout the middle of your book. First, she said – and my apologies for the swearing – they made sure their plot started with an *Oh, no!* moment. That's the inciting incident. Then the drama built to an *Oh, shit!* moment. Things are getting worse for poor old Sam. And finally, comes the *Oh, f*&k!* moment, also known as the *death moment*, the absolute low point of your story. It's as bad as it can possibly be for Fireman Sam. How will he ever save the day?

See if you can fill in the blanks for your story.

Oh, no!

Oh, shit!

Oh, f*&k!

Yes, this is a bit of fun and simplifies what is an incredibly important chunk of your novel, but if you struggled to see how you were making your character's life worse and worse, here are a few more serious tools to help with your plotting problems.

Plot formulas

Some writers plot their novels using a three-act structure. Some use a four- or five-act structure. Many writing gurus have developed formulas that break down a story into specific moments or beats or plot points. When I'm first plotting a novel, my brain resists following plotting formulas point by point. I plot more instinctively. But when I know that something with my plot isn't working, I've found it helpful to plug my plot into one of several tried-and-tested formulas and use them as diagnostic tools. I'll discuss three of my favourites in detail. (You can look online for additional story or plotting formulas you might find useful, Dan Harmon's Story Circle or Randy Ingermanson's Snowflake Method, for example.) I identify the places where my plot doesn't follow the formula, and then figure out how the plot can be reshaped to make it work.

Formula 1: Genre and obligatory scene

What is the genre of your main plot? Genres could include: action-adventure, mystery, historical, romance, fantasy, science fiction, horror, thriller and humour. Your genre creates a series of expectations in readers' minds. These are moments that your reader will intuitively expect to see in your story. If you subvert those expectations, do so for good reasons. Really young readers may not yet have developed these expectations. You might be the first romance, horror or mystery story that a young reader has ever read.

Story Grid is a great resource for writers. I've never paid for or worked through the Story Grid process from start to finish, but I do routinely download and use their genre cheat sheets. These one-pagers outline big issues your story should address based on the expected conventions of your novel, such as global value, controlling idea, core emotion, obligatory scenes, conventions and subgenres.

These cheat sheets outline the expectations your readers will have based on the genre of your book. Obligatory scenes are the key plot points that propel your story forward. For example, on the Action Story

Cheat Sheet, the first obligatory scene is 'an inciting attack by the villain'. Story Grid lists eight obligatory scenes for your action story. Do you have all of them in yours? If not, why not? Could you add these moments to your story?

You can download these cheat sheets at Story Grid: https://storygrid. com/genre-conventions/. Click on the genre of your story. This will take you to a page where you can request the cheat sheet for that genre. All you need to do is give them your email address and they will send it to you. If you'd rather not do that, a quick internet search will also lead to blogs and other resources that will share obligatory scenes for each genre.

Formula 2: Hero's journey

This is the diagnostic tool I've used the most. I loved it so much I created my own chart so I could more easily fill in the blanks (see page 75). The hero's journey is from *The Writer's Journey* by Christopher Vogler, inspired by Joseph Campbell's book *The Hero With a Thousand Faces*. Countless children's stories roughly follow this formula – from *Charlie and the Chocolate Factory* to *Harry Potter*.

Try to plug your novel into this formula. You may find that you're missing a few points. I've also found that I had the plot points but not in this order. If your plot doesn't fit neatly into these boxes, consider how you could change your plot – add or subtract scenes – to follow the hero's journey more closely.

Formula 3: Blake Snyder's Beat Sheet

Save the Cat! Strikes Back by Blake Snyder clearly and cleverly offers a step-by-step process for writing a screenplay. He outlines the 'beats' – plot points – he's discovered that many great films follow. The formula can also work for books. A quick search of the internet will yield templates and charts and loads more information on how to use Snyder's beat sheet. See if you can plug your book's beats into Snyder's Beat Sheet. Places where your plot doesn't fit are beats to add to your novel.

Free beat sheet mapper tools are available on the official Save the Cat! website: http://savethecat.com/beat-mapper.

Helpful examples dissecting current films using the beat sheet can also be found here: http://savethecat.com/beat-sheets.

Stop and consider scenes or moments to add based on your plot analysis.

We've asked some big questions in this chapter. Your responses may have identified areas that you need to focus on in your revision. Don't make any changes yet! If I have a printed manuscript, I'd use Post-it® notes to indicate where new scenes might go. Or I'd add comments in the margins of the draft on my computer. But wait until after you finish the analysis in the next chapter before diving into the changes.

Hero's journey

Step	Description	Your Story
The ordinary world	The protagonist is introduced in her/his/their ordinary world. Readers need to connect to the main character. (In children's fiction, this step can take less than a chapter, sometimes less than a paragraph.)	
Call to adventure	The moment that sets your story in motion. (This is the inciting incident mentioned earlier.)	
Refusal of the call	The protagonist – if only momentarily – rejects the call to adventure. But ultimately, the protagonist must accept the call.	
Meeting with the mentor	The protagonist, who is not yet up to the challenge, meets someone who will help her/him/them face the challenges ahead. This is usually another character, but it can be the protagonist finding the courage/resources on her/his/their own.	
Crossing the first threshold	This is the moment the protagonist leaves her/his/their ordinary world. There's no turning back. They make the leap, and the adventure begins.	
Tests, allies and enemies	The protagonist encounters emotional or physical obstacles. She/he/they will meet a variety of characters along the way – some allies, some enemies. This is when a protagonist will collect her/his/their sidekicks or team.	
Approach to the innermost cave	The protagonist and her/his/their team tackle increasingly difficult obstacles, preparing for the BIG obstacle ahead that will signal the end of the adventure.	

Ordeal	The protagonist must face her/his/their biggest fear, the antagonist or even death – perhaps literally but maybe not – and she/he/they seemingly win.	
Reward	This is a point of celebration where they claim a reward, but it doesn't necessarily mean a tangible object or treasure.	
The road back	I might also call this the 'rug pulling moment'. The protagonist believes she/he/they have won, but another obstacle, brought on by the ordeal above, must be overcome.	
Resurrection	This is the darkest moment for the protagonist. But she/he/they will rally with every ounce of strength, draw on everything they've learned and call upon their team to emerge victorious. This moment is even more satisfying if the hero overcomes the ultimate conflict in an unexpected or surprising way.	
Return with the elixir	The protagonist has earned the right to return 'home' but is a better person, who will improve her/his/their world in some way.	

This Hero's journey chart is based on the chart in *The Writer's Journey* by Christopher Vogler, in turn inspired by Joseph Campbell's book *The Hero With a Thousand Faces*.

Checklist

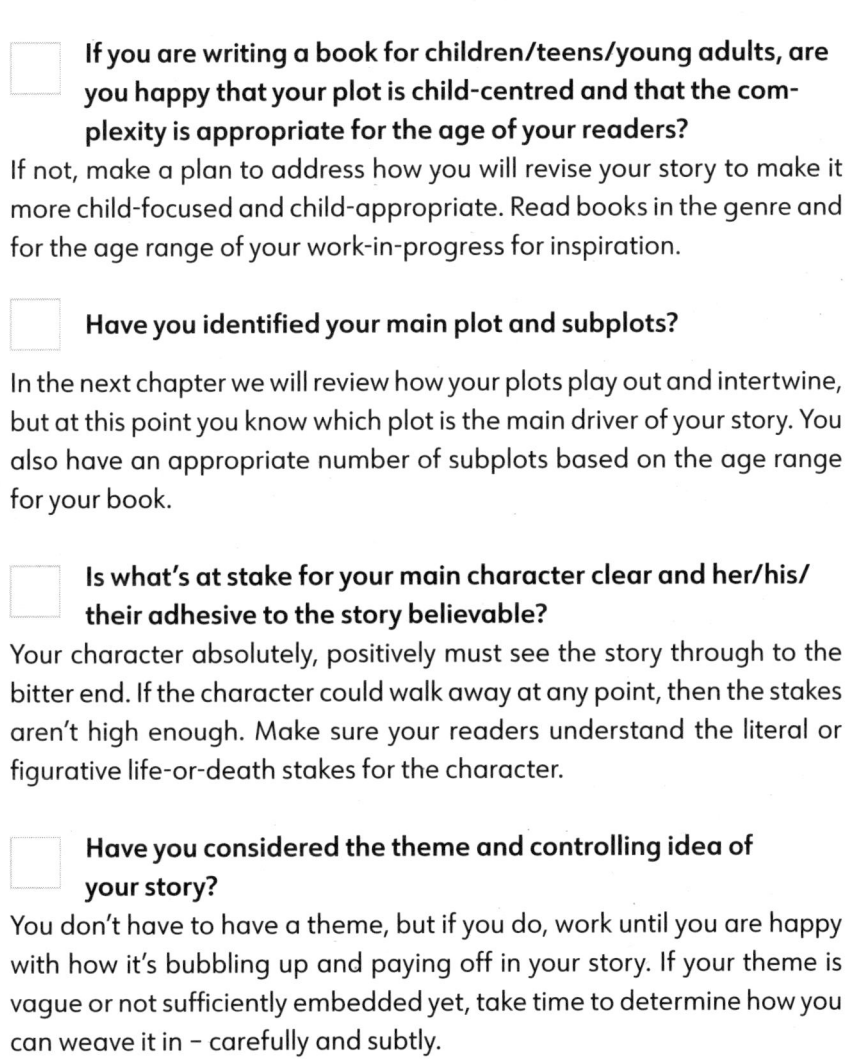

☐ **If you are writing a book for children/teens/young adults, are you happy that your plot is child-centred and that the complexity is appropriate for the age of your readers?**

If not, make a plan to address how you will revise your story to make it more child-focused and child-appropriate. Read books in the genre and for the age range of your work-in-progress for inspiration.

☐ **Have you identified your main plot and subplots?**

In the next chapter we will review how your plots play out and intertwine, but at this point you know which plot is the main driver of your story. You also have an appropriate number of subplots based on the age range for your book.

☐ **Is what's at stake for your main character clear and her/his/ their adhesive to the story believable?**

Your character absolutely, positively must see the story through to the bitter end. If the character could walk away at any point, then the stakes aren't high enough. Make sure your readers understand the literal or figurative life-or-death stakes for the character.

☐ **Have you considered the theme and controlling idea of your story?**

You don't have to have a theme, but if you do, work until you are happy with how it's bubbling up and paying off in your story. If your theme is vague or not sufficiently embedded yet, take time to determine how you can weave it in – carefully and subtly.

☐ Have you experimented with at least one of the plot formulas?

Even if you are happy with your plot, check whether any of the formulas identify trouble spots. Are you hitting all the beats and/or including any appropriate obligatory scenes? If not, why not? Does that make sense for your story? Make notes on your manuscript with possible changes. The next chapter will help you reshape your plots and subplots further chapter by chapter.

CHAPTER 4

Chapter by chapter

It's time to roll up your sleeves and consider the purpose and importance of each chapter. This series of tasks builds on your work from the previous chapter, determines how your plot and subplot are intertwined and reviews the pace of your novel. You'll rework or cut entire chapters based on what you discover.

Conscious creation

There's not one way to tell your story. I've learned a lot since *Dark Parties* was published. I have no doubt that I'd find issues large and small that I'd want to change. But I don't read my published novels that way. I read them with love for the writer I *was* and the story she felt compelled to tell. Some writers get stuck – or blocked – because they believe they must find the *perfect* way to tell a story. Perfectionism kills creativity.

What I want you to strive for is *conscious creation*. Know the story you want to tell inside and out, and then purposefully shape the reader's experience to the best of your ability. In this section, we will cast a critical eye at each chapter. Read what you've captured on the page as potential. You've already answered some questions about yourself and the story you want to tell. Let your responses inform your revision.

The exercises in this chapter were created to help you see your novel with fresh eyes. Know what you are asking of readers. You've written with wild abandon, now it's time to wrangle your idea into shape. If you are breaking literary rules, making unusual choices, do so intentionally and with good reason – *know* that you're doing it and why. I want the novel of your imagination – the experience you want to give readers – to be translated on the page. Conscious creation: that's our goal.

Structure

Let's talk a bit about the structure of your novel, which differs from your plot. As we discussed in the previous chapter, your plot is the series of events you have chosen to include in your novel arranged to enhance the drama, theme and emotion of your story. Structure is the way you lay out these moments to maximize the story experience.

Most novels for children and teens are broken into chapters, with the story told chronologically from the point of view of one main character. However, you may have discovered that this straightforward approach won't give your reader the experience you desire. For example, you might want to share multiple viewpoints or visit more than one time period. Danielle Jawando's *When Our Worlds Collided* tells the story from three points of view to demonstrate how one dramatic event changes three lives. She enhances the tension in the story by shifting from one character's viewpoint to another at key times, making you wait for resolution. Or maybe you don't think straight prose will maximize your reader's experience. *Life on the Refrigerator Door* by Alice Kulpers is told in Post-it® notes. Tia Fisher's *Crossing the Line* is told in verse.

Increasingly, writers and publishers are experimenting with innovative structures. *Invisible Emmie* by Terri Libenson intersperses a series of cartoon strips with the prose. *The Extremely Embarrassing Life of Lottie Brooks* by Katie Kirby is told in a diary format, with cartoons and drawings from the protagonist to enhance the story.

There are interactive books that must be read on devices, such as a tablet or phone. These stories blend essential or extra content in pop-ups and videos. Options could include:

- a choose your own adventure-type story where your reader decides what the protagonist does next from a list of choices

- the option to select the point of view to follow from a variety of viewpoints

- the chance to determine the order in which you read the book

- the opportunity to solve integrated puzzles and games as part of the story.

My first experience with this was the interactive e-book of *Maggot Moon* by Sally Gardner back in 2012. You can click on links in the margins for added content, including videos, animation, and historical and political information. Increasingly, publishers are finding ways to integrate different technologies into books to enhance the reader experience.

The younger the reader, the more straightforward your structure should be. However, books for younger readers have traditionally used illustrations to help readers transition from picture books and help them engage with the story. And today's younger readers are more tech-savvy and may adapt easily to new structures. Unlike adult readers, they don't have set expectations about how a book should be presented.

How do you organize and present your story?

How does your story structure enhance the reader's experience?

Do you tell it in verse or with WhatsApp messages or social media posts? If you decide to try something unusual, understand how your structural innovations might add to publication costs. For example, *Invisible Emmie* had full-colour illustrations throughout. Or if your story relies on technology, will it only be able to be sold as an e-book? This doesn't mean you shouldn't do it, but it might mean you are limiting the publishers who would consider this extra expense.

How children and teens experience story is changing as fast as the technologies available. If you think your story could benefit from an innovative structure, do some research into current options and trends in children's publishing and play with how you organize and present your story.

I love a unique structure, but only if it serves the story. In fact, structure can sometimes get in the way of a good story. It might be distracting or difficult to follow and thus take the reader out of the story. Your structure should not be a *look how clever I am* gimmick. Make sure the structure is integral to how the story unfolds, is easy to follow and enhances the tension and drama.

> **Stop and consider the structure of your story. Could there be a better way to organize your story? It's okay to play around before you settle on the final structure.**

Taking inventory

I want you to translate the plot of your novel into a five-column table. (You'll find a blank one on page 88.) You will need to make enough copies of the blank table to make a complete inventory of your book. This exercise will take you some time, but you won't regret it.

What I want you to do is simple – maybe deceptively so. All it takes is a little thought and self-discipline. Just follow these steps:

1. The first column is easy! Write the chapter number. That's it.

2. In the second column, note what happens in this chapter – not every event or action, but the most important thing that happens.

3. The next column is probably the most tricky. Why is this chapter important? Does it move the main plot along? Does it show us something important about a character? Is it a milestone for a subplot? It can do more than one thing, but fundamentally why is what we discover in this chapter important?

4. The fourth column is another easy one. How many words or pages are in this chapter?

5. And finally, how much time passes in this chapter? Is it a minute? A month? Ten years? This column could have a date and time if your novel is that specific (Thursday 11 August 1988 from 10:14 a.m. to 4 p.m.), or it could be more generic (Day 1 or even Minute 1).

Customizing your inventory

You may need to customize your inventory further if you have multiple viewpoints or if you have a unique story structure. You might add a column to indicate the point of view for each chapter. If you are not organizing your book into chapters, you can use the first column to track how you are breaking up your story. For example, if your story is told with an epistolary structure, you might have a series of dated diary entries or letters instead of chapters. Or you might insert text message exchanges – or more visual elements such as a 'wanted' poster – to move your story along. If so, you might want to add a sixth column, headed *Structure*.

Here's an example from *Chasing Danger*.

Chapter #	Action	Importance	# of words/ pages	Timeline
1	Chase is left on a floating dock in the middle of the Indian Ocean. She thinks she sees a shark, panics and almost drowns.	Learn why Chase is being sent to an isolated island with a grandma she's never met.	10 pages	January Day 1, approx 15 minutes
2	Chase travels by boat to the island. Sees vicious eels. Meets her grandma.	Discover the layout of the island and intro Artie (baddie). Foreshadow shark and eel attacks. Learn that she's determined to find out the truth about the mom who abandoned her.	12 pages	The next 30 minutes
3	Awkward exchange with aloof grandma. Snorkels in the lagoon. Collapses exhausted on deck of bungalow. Hears noise. Opens her eyes and screams.	No phone or internet connection on island. Feels rejected. See Chase is athletic and active.	11 pages	The next hour

Exercise

Your novel inventory

Fill in the table based on what happens in each chapter of your novel. If you are writing more than a phrase or two or three sentences in the Action and Importance columns, you are writing too much. This is for your eyes only, so don't worry about complete sentences. Only you need to understand what you mean.

Chapter #	Action	Importance	# of words/ pages	Timeline

Chapter #	Action	Importance	# of words/ pages	Timeline

Stop and complete a chapter-by-chapter inventory of your novel.

Evaluate your inventory

Once you've finished the inventory, review it column by column.

Action

Read down the Action column. Here's what to look for:

1. Do you have enough action? If you have a lot of chapters with talking and discussion or even researching, phone calls, texting – any passive activity – consider how you could make some of these chapters more dramatic. Be aware of too much explaining. It's necessary in any novel, but too much can make your story seem dull. The younger the reader, the faster the pace and the more drama and diversity of action you need.

2. Do you have the same action very close together? It's okay to have similar action – say, a chase – but you don't want to have these scenes too close together. Or maybe your love interests nearly kiss a few times; that's not a problem, but you might adjust the action if it happens chapter after chapter.

3. Is there a cause-and-effect relationship in the action? Does the action in one chapter lead to the action in the next? Or do you hopscotch from one coincidental action to the next? Your story can have one, perhaps even two coincidences, but after that your story may seem unbelievable. Coincidences do occur, but readers are more satisfied when they see that an occurrence wasn't a coincidence after all.

4. Have you followed through? You set expectations based on every moment and detail you include in a story. Look for places where you set expectations, and make sure those expectations are met. I always think of these as Indiana Jones payoffs. The moment I'm told in *Indiana Jones and the Raiders of the Lost Ark* that Indy has a fear of snakes, I know that he will have to face this fear – probably in a big dramatic way. If you've seen the film, you know there's a pit of

snakes waiting for him. Have you seeded secrets or lies for your main character that need to be revealed? If you set these expectations, make sure they pay off by the end of your story.

5. Is there enough conflict? Have you made it difficult enough for your character to get what she/he/they wants? Look at the obstacles you've placed in the way of your protagonist. Is there enough or too much conflict? Are the conflicts sufficiently varied?

6. Have you surprised your reader in every chapter? I don't mean a murder or explosion or mind-blowing revelation. Is there something in every chapter that will delight the reader? Your plot shouldn't be too linear. Even in romance or literary fiction, readers want a few twists, turns, conflicts and surprises.

7. Does every chapter give your reader a reason to read on? Are there any chapters where you feel you are pausing the action? If so, ask yourself if those chapters are necessary. There should be dramatic drive in every chapter. If you could lose a chapter without your reader noticing – cut it!

If you've kept your responses brief in the Action column, it can help when writing a synopsis. We'll touch on this later in the chapter.

Importance
Read down the importance column. Make sure each chapter moves the plot along and is vital to the shape of your story. In many books for young readers, the importance of the first chapter is the inciting incident. Where is your inciting incident? If it's not in the first chapter or two, why not? You may have a great reason to delay it, but make sure your opening chapters aren't merely ramping up to your story. Often writers will cut the first few chapters of a rough draft because they realise *they* needed to know what happens before the inciting incident but readers didn't.

Also look for duplication in this column. Have you cited the same importance for multiple chapters? 'Demonstrates protagonist's rebellious nature', for example. If you have a few chapters with the same importance, consider cutting one. Trust your readers to grasp a character trait or plot point the first time you share it with them.

You must be brutal. Focus solely on your readers' experience. If a chapter isn't important, delete it.

Length of chapters

Younger readers appreciate chapters that are roughly the same length. If you are writing for young adults, then you have a bit more latitude. Having extremely long or short chapters is fine, as long as you have a valid reason. If your story has an important romance, for example, you may want your readers to linger in the chapter that depicts the first kiss or intimate moment. Rather than breaking up an important scene, you want to allow your readers to savour the moment along with your young lovers. Alternatively, you may drop a bomb in a chapter – literally or figuratively – and then bolt, leaving the reader shocked with the white space and the break to let the revelation sink in.

Timeline

It's easy for the timeline to get muddled in the first draft. This exercise is a good check to make sure your chronology works. Have you accounted for weekends? If you are using actual days and months, have you looked at the calendar to make sure you've accounted for national and school holidays? If your plot requires a very specific time period, have you done your research and accounted for any significant news events where your story is set?

If you switch between time periods or tell your story out of chronological order, this is the time to check that this structure is maximizing the reader experience, not confusing the reader.

When you look at this column, review the novel's time-versus-space ratio. Does one day get three chapters while an entire year passes in one chapter? It's not necessarily a problem, just make sure it's a conscious decision and serves your story.

Exercise

Genre milestones

We're not quite finished with your inventory. Grab your highlighters or use the highlight function in your word processing software, if you've created your inventory electronically. And highlight each of the following in a different colour on your table.

Highlight for genre. Based on the genre of your book, highlight key moments and/or obligatory scenes for your main plot. So, if you are writing romance, highlight romantic moments. Maybe it's a look or a touch and obviously the kiss. If you are writing a mystery, note your clues and red herrings. If it's action-adventure, where's the action? If it's scary, where are your frights? If it's funny, where are your laughs? Now analyse your inventory based on genre. When I did this for an early draft of the first book in my action-adventure series *Chasing Danger*, I realized that I didn't have enough action. Are you giving readers what they will expect based on genre?

Highlight turning points. Place an asterisk by the greatest emotional moments, turning points and epiphanies.

Highlight subplots. Find a different colour for each of your subplots and colour-code key moments in each subplot.

Review your inventory again. Based on what you've highlighted, determine whether your plot and subplot points are spread evenly throughout. If not, why not? If a subplot is important, you want to keep it in the mind of your reader. If you find that a subplot springs up in only a few places, you might want to consider either enhancing it or removing it.

Are the key moments in your plot and subplot clear? Are you happy with where they appear in your novel? Have you resolved them all by the end? If not, why not? Will it frustrate or excite your reader? In books for adults and young adults, it's okay not to tie up every loose end. In books for middle grade and younger, you may want to resolve most issues before the end. Obviously, it's fine to leave a few loose ends if you are hoping for a sequel or setting up a series.

Exercise

Graph your story

When I give my revision workshop, this exercise is one that writers either find really helpful or just don't understand. This is for those who are visual learners.

Grab some graph paper and enough coloured pens or pencils for your main plot and any significant subplots. Create a graph with chapter numbers along the horizontal axis at the bottom. The vertical axis, which you can number or leave blank, measures tension or drama.

First, plot your main plot on the graph. Show the rising and falling tension as the stakes get higher and the tension mounts. The highest point will be your climax. Do the same for all your subplots. This is not an exact science. Don't get too hung up on the exact vertical plot points, use your gut to tell you how much the tension or drama is increasing.

Your graph should look something like this. It's a visual representation of the drama in your novel.

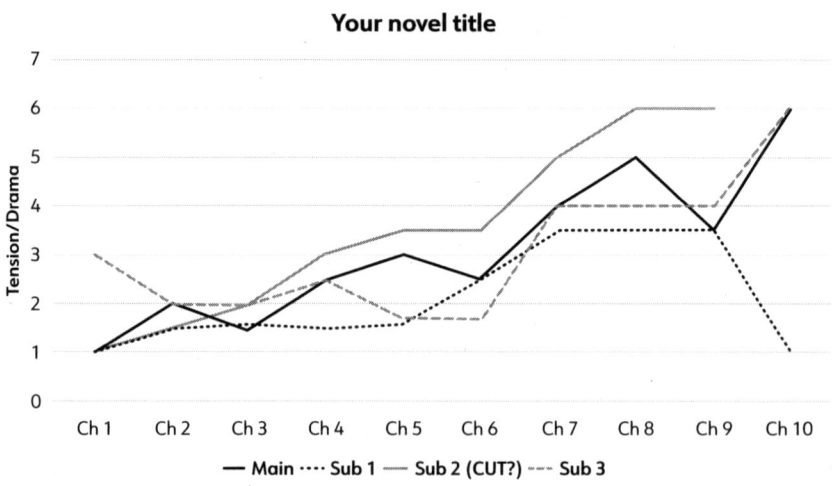

What you should see is that your main and subplots are connected with one another. One's high point might be another's low. All of the subplots should intersect with the main plot. If you look at subplot 2 in the graph, you'll note that it initially ties closely to the other plots but then jets off, completely untouched by the main or subplots. If you have something similar, consider cutting this subplot. You will find it won't be that difficult because it's not intricately tied to the main plot.

Also look for flat lines. These indicate a plot with limited tension or drama. You will naturally have some plateaus, but do they last too long? You might look for ways to heighten the tension of this plot, or you could decide it's unnecessary.

Are you happy with how the graph looks – how your plots are connected? If not, what would your ideal graph look like? Do you need more action and drama earlier in the story? Does your plot sag around the middle? Make notes on how to adjust your plot and subplots based on what you discovered.

For inspiration

If the exercises in this chapter have made you realize that your plot or subplots are lacking, create an inventory for and/or graph a favourite book or film. It might be most helpful if the book or film you select for inspiration is in the same genre and age range as your work-in-progress.

In my last class as a student at Goldsmiths' masters course on creative and life writing, one of my fellow students – feeling bereft at the end of our formal education – asked our tutor, author Pamela Johnson, how would we cope without her guidance and inspiration. Johnson said that all the teachers we would ever need are on the shelves of bookshops and libraries. So whenever I need inspiration, I remember her words and find my own personal mentor in the pages of a book.

When I was writing for young adults, I dissected *A Gathering Light* by Jennifer Donnelly. I adore this book. It's a book for writers and lovers of words. It's about 17-year-old Mattie, who dreams of being a writer but isn't sure how that will ever happen. Teenage Sara Grant had the same dream and worry. I am also from the Midwestern United States not far from where the book is set. This book spoke to me. It's also a mystery. I won't give too much away in case you ever want to read it. I reread it with a pencil in my hand and a notebook by my side. I counted nine subplots and studied how Donnelly had crafted a novel that kept me turning pages without confusing me – in fact, inspiring and delighting me. Once I'd revealed how she wove her magic, I considered how I could create similar magic in my own work.

When working on an earlier draft of *Chasing Danger*, I felt that my tale of action and adventure wasn't exciting enough. One of my all-time favourite action-adventure films is *Die Hard*. We can argue whether it's a Christmas film, but you can't deny it's a stonking story that has you cheering for John McClane and keeps you on the edge of your seat until the rousing end.

I love a writing exercise where I can read or watch a great story and call it work. On an eight-hour flight, I watched *Die Hard* on my iPad with pencil in my hand and blank notebook. I stopped and started the film jotting down every plot point – every beat – of the film. Next, I compared *Chasing Danger*'s inventory and graph with *Die Hard*'s. Where were the similarities? Where were the differences? How could I give *Chasing Danger* readers an experience that rivalled the excitement in *Die Hard*?

I revised *Chasing Danger*, based on what I learned from analysing the film. I don't want to spoil either story for you, but I love the twist in *Die Hard*. Spoiler alert: The terrorist plot in *Die Hard* turns out to be a cover for a multimillion-dollar heist. I crafted a similar twist in *Chasing Danger*. After that, I thought of *Chasing Danger* as: *Die Hard* on a desert island.

Exercise

Write your synopsis

Once you are happy with the shape of your story and your readers' experience, a good test is to write a one-page synopsis. It won't be easy. If I'm honest, I'd rather write another novel then try to squeeze my intricately plotted novel with a host of intriguing characters into one page. It feels impossible.

Your completed inventory should help. Use the action column as the spine of your synopsis. Start with bullet points of your main plot. Tease in your subplots, knowing that you probably can't include them all. You want to show your main character's emotional journey, but you won't be able to mention every character. A rough rule of thumb is to share the inciting incident, three key plot points, the climax and the conclusion. Do include spoilers! An agent wants to know if the ending pays off on the promise you've set up in your opening chapters.

A few pointers:

- Smooth your key milestones into a narrative. Not *this happens and then this happens*; rather, *this happens and therefore this happens*. Show action and reaction.

- Try to suggest the novel's tone or voice. If your novel is funny, try to demonstrate that in your synopsis. If it's a mystery, weave in intrigue.

- Make sure important characters appear – but not every character.

- You will have to summarize: for example, our hero tries and fails to find the location of the secret cave.

- Your synopsis is a professional document, so don't be cute or gimmicky. It is meant to be read by interested agents and editors. It must demonstrate that you know how to plot a novel.

- In my opinion, you should avoid stating the themes or lessons of your story. *This is a story about climate change and how we all have a personal stake in saving our planet.* NO! Themes and lessons should bubble up from the story. Children go to school to learn lessons. Books should be more subtle and allow young readers to think for themselves.

Writing a synopsis can also flag up plot problems. (I often try to write a synopsis very early in my development process: it's easier to write a one-pager when you haven't yet figured out every twist, turn and surprise.) Look out for plots that aren't clear. Maybe there's no real conflict, too *much* action – or not enough. Watch out for uninteresting characters, as well as for passive narrators or plot that *happens* to your character instead of being *driven* by your character. Make sure your main character is at the heart of the conflict and can/will resolve it.

Years ago I went to a synopsis-writing workshop. I was trying to write a synopsis for a story I was maybe 150 pages into. I really struggled. What I realized was that I didn't have a clear vision for the story. I had great characters, an interesting setting, a collection of engaging scenes and an issue I wanted to explore, but I couldn't synopsize it because I didn't have a coherent plot.

Stop and revise your novel. You should edit until you are happy with the shape, pace and drama of your story.

Checklist

☐ **Are you happy with the overall shape of your novel?**

You've cut unnecessary chapters and improved the pace of your story as well as orchestrated how the drama will unfold.

☐ **Have you selected a structure that maximizes reader experience?**

It's not too late to experiment with a different structure – shifting perspectives and timelines, for example – or play with the format to create an enhanced, interactive or high-tech book.

☐ **Are your main plot and subplots tied tightly together?**

You've removed distracting subplots that weren't adding to the reader experience and enhanced those subplots that weren't working hard enough.

CHAPTER 5

Scene by scene

At this point in your revision, you should be happy with the overall structure of your novel, how your action plays out chapter by chapter and the arc of your characters' journeys. Now we drill down and review each scene in detail. Is each scene vital and building to a satisfying conclusion? You will disassemble the key moments of your novel and discover how you breathe life into each and every scene.

Identifying a scene

What is a scene? If your book were made into a film, the director would delineate each scene by fading in at the start and fading out to signal its end. A scene change is how we transition from place to place, note a shift in time, create tension or give the reader a moment's break. I think of each scene as a mini story. It has a beginning, a middle and an end. You will need to draw your reader in, guide them through the action and emotion and then satisfactorily end each scene, giving the reader a reason to read on. Each scene should build on the previous and set the stage for the next.

As we did for each chapter, we will consider the action and purpose of each scene. Writers should try to make each scene as tight as possible. Scenes are like awkward family obligations – your spouse's cousin Debbie's third child's christening, for example. You want to arrive as late as possible and leave as early as you can. If the purpose of the scene is a dramatic fight between two best friends at a house party, you don't need to show us how your protagonist prepared for or travelled to the party. You might want to start with her weaving through the partygoers and seeing her boyfriend lip-locked with her friend. After a heated confrontation, give your main character the final word and end the scene. Again, we don't need to see her storming out the door and muttering all the way to the bus stop. Maximize the drama of the moment and move on.

Our job as writers is not to tell readers *everything*. You aren't a sports commentator giving an excruciatingly detailed play by play. Your job is to select key moments and breathe life into them. Sometimes we tell our readers too much or share something too soon. We know the backstory and the future of our characters, which can lead to oversharing. We should ask ourselves: ***What do my readers need to know and when do they need to know it?*** It's a question I write on manuscript critiques often. You know that your character is an alien or had a traumatic experience two years ago, but do you need to reveal this to your readers right here and right now? What you withhold is as important as what you share.

I remember explaining this level of scene-by-scene scrutiny to a student in my master's-level course on writing for children. She looked at me as if I had lost my mind. 'That's hard work,' she said, somehow surprised. Yes, my fellow writers, it *is* hard work. No one said writing a novel would be easy, but this is one of the most satisfying bits. This level of care separates a good novel from a great one. You've mapped out your journey, now we must interrogate every stop along the way.

Breathing life into a scene

Show, don't tell! If you've ever taken a class or read a book on creative writing, you've heard this edict before. (And I've mentioned it already when we discussed theme.) Writers who fully grasp what this means give readers the best experience. Indulge me in a quick review of this principle.

- Telling = summarizing the action. We know what happens, but the scene is not played out on the page so we can't see it in our mind's eye like a film.

- Showing = allowing readers to fully experience the scene moment by moment. Readers are immersed in the scene.

Malorie Blackman masters the art of showing in *Noughts & Crosses* (Doubleday, 2001). In Chapter 1, Blackman sets up the relationship between Callum and Sephy perfectly by deftly showing their awkward first kiss. If Blackman *told* her readers what happened in the scene, it would go something like this:

> Callum convinces a reluctant Sephy, his best friend, to kiss him to see what it's like. After a few bumpy attempts, they kiss properly. Sephy feels attracted to Callum.

We know what happens in the scene, but there's no energy or electricity when I tell what happens.

Blackman spends three glorious pages bringing this pivotal moment to life. Here's a little taste of that scene:

> Before I could change my mind, Callum's lips were already on mine – and just as soft and gentle as before. His tongue flicked into my mouth again. After a brief moment of thinking ugh! I found that it wasn't too bad. In fact it was actually quite nice in a gross-to-think-about-but-OK-to-do sort of way.

As you review your novel scene by scene, look out for places where you summarize the action. Does each key moment spring to life on the page?

Orientation

Your aim is to seamlessly move your readers from scene to scene. I call this orienting your readers. Where are they in time and space? In one scene we can be in outer space in the year 2150 and in the next, return your reader to the present day. The younger the reader, the more you will need to signpost these changes. You want your reader to be immersed in your story, not wondering where and when it's taking place.

In the next exercise, you will review how and when you orient your readers in each scene. It will help you subtly shepherd your readers from one dramatic moment to the next.

Exercise

Analysing each scene

This exercise was inspired by one in Darcy Pattison's *Novel Metamorphosis: Uncommon Ways to Revise*. It's a wonderful workbook – and it sparked my love for revision.

Here's the step-by-step process I use to analyse each scene:

1. Place a box around each scene. That's it. I prefer to use a coloured pen on a printed copy of my manuscript. (One with an eraser if you can find it – just in case you make a mistake.) You can also do this by inserting a shape using the *Draw* function of your word-processing software. Do this for every single scene in your book.

2. In the margins by each box, note:

    Orientation: When and where does the scene take place? Example: the next day, in Brooke's back garden or a few minutes later in the school corridor.

    Action: What happens in the scene? Example: Mia confesses her love for Dominic. Mason is chased and narrowly escapes the bad guy.

    Purpose: Why is this scene important? Why does it need to be here? Example: It shows Evie's fear of the dark or it reveals a vital clue to solve the mystery.

EXERCISE IN ACTION

This is an example of how to analyse each scene. The text is from the opening of *Magic Mansion*, the sixth and final book in my *Magic Trix* series.

Creeping cats! Trix's world had been turned upside down. Really and truly!

She was dangling like a bat from the chandelier in Magic Mansion's grand ballroom. All the witches in the Sisterhood of Magic were gathered below her. Their eyes and tiaras twinkled up at her. The chandelier's crystals jingled and jangled like chimes in a hurricane as she swung back and forth in time to the orchestra's music – and the gasps of the crowd.

She bent her knees to grip the chandelier, but she could feel herself slipping. What had started as an enchanted adventure was ending as a nightmare.

Her beautiful yellow ballgown, which had once shimmered like the summer sun, was in tatters. She was missing one of her shoes and Jinx, her magical familiar, was hanging by a paw from the hem of her gown.

Tonight should have been the most magical night of her life, but it had gone terribly wrong. Trix loved being a witch. She had tried her best to learn everything her magical tutor, Lulu, had taught her. She had practised her spells and flying and potions like a good witch-in-training but, no matter how hard she tried, she seemed to be the very best at making magical messes. And *this* was the most spectacular super-duper mess of them all.

Meow! Jinx cried, his claw etching tracks in the silky fabric as he inched lower and lower.

I endeavour to draw readers in with a little intrigue and mystery.

Orientation: This line tells you exactly where the protagonist is.

Building atmosphere.

Because this is book six, I needed to give a recap for my young readers or any readers new to the series.

Action: Trix is hanging upside down and saves her magical cat familiar Jinx. She's struggling to think of a way to save herself from falling and ending her utter humiliation.

"Hold on, Jinx," Trix called, catching the black and white kitten as the last threads of her hem gave way.

She held Jinx close and felt the thrum of his purrs. "How are we ever going to get out of this mess?" she whispered.

A smile tugged at the edges of Trix's lips. She had to admit that she must look silly up here. She liked hanging upside down on the climbing frame at school – the way it made her tummy flutter and her head feel fuzzy. This might even have been fun – if everyone from the Sisterhood of Magic wasn't staring at her in shock and horror, *and* if she couldn't see Stella smugly smirking, *and* if Trix didn't feel her grip on the chandelier loosening.

She had almost forgotten she was a witch. All she needed was the right spell to keep her from falling, repair her dress and erase everyone's memory of this oh-so-embarrassing moment, but that type of magic was very big for a little witch-in-training.

She couldn't let go of Jinx, and her brain couldn't think of a word that rhymed with upside down or right-side up!

Creeping cats!

How had tonight gone so topsy-turvy? It had started so wonderfully, with an unexpected invitation.

This scene is less than 500 words and covers only a few minutes. This is the entire first chapter of the book. With younger readers, I tend to have one scene per chapter.

Purpose: This is both the opening and climatic scene of the novel. It's meant to re-introduce the world and Trix, Jinx and the key cast of characters from the previous five books. I wanted to start with a outrageous and funny moment so my readers would wonder how poor Trix had managed to end up in this precarious situation.

Orientation: This is the opening scene of the novel. This line tells you that this is the end of the night and that we are about to rewind and show you the story from the beginning.

I end the scene on a cliffhanger. How will Trix ever get out of this mess?

What did you discover?

Once you've placed a box around each scene and noted orientation, action and purpose, review your draft considering the following ten points.

1. Look at the number and size of boxes per chapter.

You might only have one scene per chapter. There's no rule on how many scenes you should have in a chapter, but you are setting expectations for your reader. The younger the reader, the more they will appreciate consistency.

Notice how your scenes vary. Are they all roughly the same size? Scrutinize scenes that are much longer or shorter than the rest. Just as we did with chapter lengths, know the unconscious rules you are creating for your reader. Maybe pivotal scenes are longer because you want your reader to linger in these moments. Maybe you throw in a shorter scene to grab the reader's attention and surprise them in some way. Too many short scenes may indicate that you aren't allowing your readers to fully experience the key moments you've selected.

If you have chunks of text that fall outside a scene, that's okay. These can be necessary explanatory transitions or narrator asides. But do double-check. Are they necessary? Do they add to the reader experience?

2. Have you oriented your reader in each scene?

Your readers should easily transition between scenes and know where they are in time and space. You can quickly fix this if necessary. However, you don't need to do this in the first line or in an explanatory manner – unless you are playing with tropes or poking fun at older storytelling traditions. *It was a dark and stormy night in Central London in 1861.* Some writers orient readers with a subhead at the beginning of each chapter, especially if they are changing character perspectives or locations. For example, you might have a headline under each chapter with something like: *Lorna, Edinburgh, 2010.*

Do you orient your reader the same way in each scene? For example, do you start with a phrase such as *The next day*? Or do you start with a description of the setting? Neither is wrong, but if you do it the same way with too many scenes, your writing can begin to feel formulaic. Also, though orientation is vital, it's not the most important thing. It doesn't have to come first. For inspiration, look at ways your favourite authors weave orientation into each scene.

3. Have you drawn your readers into each scene?

Each scene needs to lure us in. A snappy piece of dialogue can do this, but so can building atmosphere with description. Readers want to know what happens next, but try to vary how you entice them into a scene.

4. How do you leave us at the end of each scene?

Some writers will assign a + or – to the end of each scene. Do you end on a high note with the scene's situation or problem favourably resolved? Do you end on a cliffhanger? Do you end on a low note, with readers unsure how your protagonist will ever get out of this situation? Keep your readers guessing. Don't train them to expect a certain outcome at the end of every scene. The key is to give your readers a reason to read on.

5. Is each scene as tight as it could be?

Consider if you are starting and ending your scenes in the right places. Could you start later or end sooner and not lose the dramatic impact to the scene? If so, cut these moments of ramping up or fizzling out.

6. Have you selected the best setting for each scene?

Note the location of each scene. In a first draft, I often find that I have too much action happening in one location. You aren't creating a film – yet – so each location costs nothing extra. If you are trying to create a claustrophobic atmosphere, then setting many scenes in the same place is a strategic decision. If not, vary the location of your scenes.

7. Does each location maximize the drama?

Why is the scene happening here? What does the location add to the scene? In an early draft of *Dark Parties*, several scenes were set in my teen girl's bedroom. It was realistic for Neva to chat with her mum or best friend tucked away cozily in her room, but it stifled the atmosphere and often added nothing to the drama. I moved one of the scenes to a graveyard and another to a park on a merry-go-round at night – for good reason and to make the most of my dystopian setting. This shift in scenery really added to the drama.

8. Do the chronology and pace make the most sense?

Is every scene one day or one minute? Is this intentional? Do you start slowly, with each scene covering roughly the same amount of time and over the course of a chapter or the novel shift to shorter or longer time periods for a scene? If so, why? Does that make sense for your story? Are you rushing the action, or does your pace make the story drag? You need to find the proper pace – as Goldilocks might say, the one that feels *just right*.

9. Review the action in each scene.

We did this when we reviewed each chapter. Do you have too much or too little action? Do you have similar action in too many scenes? Look for passive scenes. If words such as *tells* and *explains* are used when describing the action or purpose of the scene, perhaps not much is happening in this scene. Are you pushing pause to tell your readers important information? How can you show them instead? We'll cover how to turn your telling into showing in a later chapter, where you'll review your work sentence by sentence.

10. What's the purpose of each scene?

As you did above, look for duplication of purpose. Are too many scenes trying to do the same thing? Are they all necessary? Make them work harder or cut them entirely.

Make sure each scene is more than what happens next. Each scene must be vital to your story's experience. Does each moment advance your plot or subplots, reveal your character or subtly enhance your theme? The younger your audience, the less time/space you will have. Make sure that every scene is vital and that it encourages your readers to turn the page.

Stop and cut entire scenes if they aren't pulling their weight. If you can cut a scene and it will not be missed by your readers, by all means cut it!

Setting and atmosphere

The setting of your novel should inform your plot and your characters. I used to think that setting didn't matter. You need a page-turning plot and authentic characters, but where it happened – that was just the backdrop. I thought of it as a stage play – with sets crafted to give the shallow illusion of place. But in a novel, you need to go beyond *telling* your readers where they are in time and space. You must help them experience it.

I used to set my stories in Anytown, USA. I was from a small town. It's what I knew best. With each of these early stories, I could have picked up the story and moved it to another location and it wouldn't have mattered much. That's because my story wasn't immersed in the setting. I quickly learned that setting matters a great deal. If your story could happen anywhere else, your setting isn't working hard enough.

I've written books set on a desert island, in a fictional English village, at an ice hotel inside the Arctic Circle, in a dystopian country, and in a claustrophobic bunker deep in a mountain outside Las Vegas. I researched each setting as best I could. I visited the location if it was economically feasible and took loads of notes and videos. If I couldn't afford to visit it, I would read travel books, watch clips or films and ask experts or people who had lived or visited there.

If the setting was imaginary, I'd spend a lot of time crafting it. I would create maps and a separate document, which would explain the history as well as the social and political background of my imaginary place. Some writers create mood boards where they collect images to help them visualise the setting. I'd develop historical timelines. I'd find places that were similar to what I'd imagined and research those places and times.

If you haven't done a deep-dive into your setting, stop and do more research. How will you weave this rich detail into your story?

Exercise

Justify your setting

Is your setting working hard enough? Does it enhance your story? If your novel has more than one significant setting, you will want to answer these questions for each important setting.

What is the overall setting for your story? What place and time?

Is your story set in a particular city at a particular period in time? If your setting is imaginary, then you will have a lot more work to do. Explain your setting and how it's different from the real world.

How does your setting influence your characters?

Here are a few examples of what I mean:

1. How do your characters speak? Not only what language and/or dialect, but what words they choose and colloquialisms and slang will be influenced by location – and can quickly date a book. As an American who has lived in the UK for over twenty years, I'm keenly aware that we are two countries separated by a common language. I once told my mother-in-law that I was going to wear pants to a special occasion. In the UK pants = underwear. In the US, pants = trousers. Language also changes regionally. The majority of Americans call a fizzy drink *soda*, but Midwesterners call it *pop*. I grew up calling a green pepper a *mango*. I didn't know there was such a thing as a mango *fruit* until well into my adult years. Make sure you've nailed the language of your characters.

2. In *Dark Parties'* fictional Homeland, I had to eliminate any phrases or references to foreign countries or languages because my protagonist had grown up believing that there was nothing outside her

protected, domed country. I also had to eliminate any mention of 'globe' or 'world'. It was surprising how often these words are part of common phrases.

3. How does your location influence your characters' dreams and aspirations? I grew up in a small town. My dad always said it was like living in a fishbowl. I'm a rule-follower to this day because there were always too many eyes and ears on me when I was growing up. If I stepped out of line, I was always caught! In *Dark Parties*, my claustrophobic Homeland limited my protagonist's hopes and dreams because the sky inside the dome was literally the limit.

How does your setting enhance your plot, create obstacles/opportunities or provide atmosphere?

In my action-adventure series *Chasing Danger*, I made liberal use of glamorous foreign locations. From run-away dogsleds to dead bodies in blocks of ice, *Mystery at the Ice Hotel* made the most of its unique setting. What happens in your story that could only take place in the setting you've selected? List any obstacles or opportunities that your setting affords. Does your setting create conflict for your character, for example?

I hope you've discovered the reasons that your story can take place only in the location(s) you've selected. If you haven't made the most of your setting, now's the time to pause and outline how you will maximize your setting in the next draft.

Exercise

Senses test

If you find your setting isn't coming to life or you have minimal description of your setting, run the senses test on each scene.

- What do you see?
- What do you hear?
- What do you smell?
- What does the character touch?
- And if appropriate, what does the character taste?

You probably won't cover all five in each scene. Also, if you use the same location more than once, you won't need the same level of description. You might note only if something has changed at this location since we last visited it.

Writers typically draw on sight and sound, but don't forget your other senses. The sense of smell can be very evocative: it's the sense tied most closely to memory. Make sure that the details you select are working hard enough. Try to help the reader experience the location. Generic descriptions – *rundown house* or *bad smell*, for example – don't really help your reader to see or smell what your character is experiencing. Does the house have peeling paint or boarded-up windows? Is the smell like a rotten egg? Unwashed gym socks? Be as specific and concrete as you can.

Each detail can do more than set the scene. The details your protagonist or narrator chooses to show readers can reveal something about the character or her/his/their feelings. A depressed character may see only the clouds and shadows. Your observant detective will notice the minute details that will help solve the crime. To demonstrate your character's optimism, they may focus on the brightening horizon instead of the flash of lightning.

Adding sensory detail can help build tension and create atmosphere in a scene. It's important to include, but make sure it doesn't slow your pace or overshadow your character.

Checklist

☐ **Are you satisfied that each scene is necessary and, in this particular order, provides the right pace and shape for your story?**
You've picked the key moments to reveal your story and brought them to life. You've cut unnecessary scenes and enhanced scenes that weren't working hard enough.

☐ **Have you oriented and delighted your readers in each scene, leading them seamlessly through the story and giving them a reason to read on?**
If not, take the time to revise each and every scene until you are happy with the scene length and that the drama unfolds on the page to keep readers hooked and draw them into the next scene.

☐ **Is your overall setting integral to the story?**

Your story simply couldn't happen anywhere else. You've made the most of your setting and provided sensory detail to help your readers experience – not just be told – the location of each scene.

CHAPTER 6

Honing voice

A distinctive voice is what separates competent stories from publishable ones. Every agent and editor – and every reader, for that matter – searches for a fresh voice that springs off the page. It's easy to spot books with a distinctive voice, but it's difficult to help writers understand and hone the voice of their novel. This chapter is going to do just that.

What is voice?

Voice is the combination of your personal, character and narrator voices. It's the sum of all the decisions you make – big or small, conscious or unconscious – when writing a story. Your objective with each piece of writing is to find an original voice that is perfect for the story you want to tell. Sounds simple, but it's probably the most elusive aspect of writing. It's the bit that's difficult to teach. I've heard some agents, editors and published authors say writers either have it or they don't. I don't believe that. I'm going to try my best to explain voice and help you uncover it in your writing.

The best definition of voice – the moment voice really clicked in my brain – was from Sarah Davies, a retired literary agent and former publishing director at Macmillan Children's Books UK, in a presentation she gave entitled 'The Magic of Voice'. I've heard it many times – because I repeatedly asked her to give it at retreats and to the master's class I taught. She described voice using the analogy of music. Artists can sing the same song, but you can tell within a few seconds whether it's Bruce Springsteen or Taylor Swift. And it's more than the fact that we recognize their voices. It's the tone, quality, range, phrasing and interpretation of the song. To quote nearly every judge on *X Factor* when critiquing a promising contestant, it's how they make a song uniquely their own.

In Beyoncé's 2024 country album, *Cowboy Carter*, she covered Dolly Parton's song *Jolene*, originally released in 1973. If you haven't done so already, listen to both versions. Two very different artists; two very different interpretations. In Dolly's original, she begs Jolene not to take her man. Beyoncé, however, while drawing on the same melody and similar words, isn't pleading; she's *warning* Jolene that she'd better not take her man. It's essentially the same song, but the experience couldn't be more different.

Finding your voice

The good news is that each of us already has a unique voice. No one sees the world quite like you do. You are who you are because of nature and nurture. Everything you've experienced, everything you've learned, every person you've met – absolutely everything up until this minute, has formed your personality and made you, well, *you*. And when you are developing your protagonists, consider as much as you can about what makes them *them*. Knowing yourself and knowing your main character is the first step to bringing a distinctive voice to your work.

We all have a style that comes naturally. Finding the stories that work with your innate style can be one way to bring voice to your piece. If you naturally write with a bouncy, fun style, writing a serious drama might be a struggle. Does your current work-in-progress sit snugly in your comfort zone? It's fantastic to challenge ourselves as writers, so it's fine if the answer is *no*.

Every piece of writing has a voice. Unfortunately, many authors write in a flat voice. It's not distinctive, original or memorable. There's nothing wrong with their sentence structure or word choice, but the writing – to continue with our music analogy – just doesn't sing. It's readable but not captivating. The key is to craft an original and appropriate voice for your story.

Ironically, I struggled to find the right voice for this book at first. When I started drafting the proposal, I reverted back to my uni term-paper voice – very formal and official. That's what experts sound like, right? Well, not me. It took some experimenting and practice to – and this might sound crazy – write in my own conversational voice. I'm so used to slipping under the skin of my characters and finding their various voices, that allowing myself to chat on the page in my own voice took some time. I had to find the right balance. I didn't want to be too chatty and informal, but I wanted my personality to come through on the page.

Let's use the previous paragraph to demonstrate voice. First, I considered my audience. This book is for writers who have finished a draft of a novel. I assume a level of expertise in writing and a knowledge of the publishing industry. My vocabulary should reflect this. Next, I looked at the character of the piece – aka me! I wanted an approachable style. How do I reflect all of this in the previous paragraph?

Answer: First it comes through in my sentence structure. I use a few short sentences for emphasis and punch among longer sentences. I also love a dash or an aside. There are a few scattered in the paragraph – 'and this might sound crazy,' for example. I ask questions to engage you in a discussion and I hope, draw you in. You can see that my choice of words is more casual. For example, my use of 'uni' and 'chatty'.

Expectations and Influences

First, think about how your intended readership should influence your writing. We touched on this in earlier chapters, but I want you to consider how you shape the voice of your piece to suit your readers. There's an added complexity to consider if you are writing for children and young adults.

What is the age of your readership?

If you are writing for very young readers, you will need to consider word choice carefully. What words can your readers sound out and read? Will they know the meaning of the word? If not, how will you help them understand its meaning in the context of the story? Look at your sentence structure and length. Shorter and more straightforward sentences are better for young readers. The older your reader, the better they can cope with complexity.

One mistake writers for children often make is to unconsciously give their characters their own adult personal traits. A young protagonist, for example, is described as a 10 year-old but somehow demonstrates the knowledge, experience or sophistication of the adult writer. Review the thoughts and feelings of your main characters and make sure they are age-appropriate. As you continue to consider the voice of your story, don't forget you are writing for readers whose life experiences are far more limited than yours.

If you are writing for adults, you should still consider your readership, not necessarily their age, but where do you want to pitch your story in terms of sophistication and complexity. Do you want your prose to be at the literary end of the spectrum? Or do you want your novel to be more accessible and conversational?

Point of view

The point of view you've chosen, in part, determines the voice of the story. Just a quick recap of what I mean by point of view. If you've chosen first person, you've selected the best person from your cast of characters to reveal the story. We will see the world through her/his/their eyes. A close-third-person narrative is similar, but it's 'she/he/they' rather than 'I'. Both are intimate perspectives. With first, we are typically in the head of the most important character. With close-third, we can dip into the head of the main character, but there's a slight distance. In writing for children, these are the two most popular choices.

With first person, the voice in the piece is solely the voice of the main character, except dialogue from other characters. With the other options, you will not only have the voice of your character or characters, but also the voice of the narrator.

The omniscient point of view is often described as the 'God perspective' – all-knowing and all-seeing. With an omniscient point of view, the narrator is able to head-hop – that is, give the internal point of view from any character. This may work for older readers but could be confusing to middle grade and younger readers. The omniscient point of view used to be more popular in children's books, such as in the fairytales that started with 'Once upon a time'. Some writers naturally slip into this storytelling voice, but an omniscient viewpoint creates distance between the story and the reader. It often holds readers at arm's length and *tells* the story rather than allowing readers to experience it.

I won't spend much time on second-person (you) prospective. This mostly is reserved for young adult and adult novels. Younger readers will have difficulty understanding this perspective. If you want to deploy this perspective, do so because it's the best way to share your stories with readers – not as a party trick or to show off.

Exercise

Consider point of view

Just do a quick diagnostic of the point of view in your story.

What point of view have you selected?

If you are using first or a close-third perspectives, the voice of your piece will most likely be your character's voice. If you selected third or omniscient, you are creating a narrator's voice. You'll need to answer a few more questions:

Who is the narrator?

Why is this person telling the story?

Sometimes the narrator will talk directly to the reader. I've seen this mostly in funny stories. Look at Anna Brooke's *Monster Bogey* for a fun (albeit gross) example of this. Chapter 1 starts with the narrator asking you, the reader, if you have ever picked your nose? A perfectly legit question for a novel for 7- to 9-year-olds. But the main character in the story is Frank Bear Horace Pickerty-Boop.

Why have you chosen this perspective?

What does it add to your story?

If you aren't sure why you chose a particular point of view or what it adds, now might be the time to experiment with the point of view of your piece.

Exercise

Play with point of view

If you find that the voice in your piece is falling flat and you are writing in something other than first person, try shifting to first – really dive inside the mind and body of your main character. This can sometimes add the personality that your writing is lacking. Then shift back to a close-third person, if that's what you think your story demands.

Present or past tense?

A quick note on tense. Writers often have a tense with which they feel more comfortable. Most children's books are written in the past tense, which means that the action has already happened. However, you want the story to have happened recently so that the voice of your narration is still close to the age of your protagonist – and the age of the reader. In the past tense, you still can comment on what is about to happen. For example, *little did Jenny know that an ice cream cone could change her life*. If your perspective is too distant – that of an adult looking back fondly at a childhood experience with the wisdom and hindsight of an adult – what you might be writing is a book for adult readers. (We discussed this in more depth in Chapter 1 in the section on 'The added responsibility of writing for children'.)

I'm fond of writing in the present tense, which is what a growing number of writers are using for young adult fiction. I like the immediacy of it. The story is happening in real time, so the reader is experiencing the action alongside the main character. This adds a level of excitement and intensity. If the story is in past tense, you can reasonably assume that the main character has lived to tell the tale. With present tense, anything can happen. If your story feels sluggish, it might be worth experimenting with the present tense.

Practise, practise, practise

For some writers, voice comes naturally. They have that rare gift of effortlessly creating a voice on the page. I don't think they were born that way, though. I think they've filled their brains with beautiful music, books, poetry, art and life experiences. Like actors, these writers find it easy to assume a role or identity that is not their own and transcribe this character's voice to the page. If you are one of these, I'm so happy for you. Am I jealous? Sure! The rest of us have to work for it.

Early on in my writing career, I had to work hard to break the bad habits I learned in school. You remember when you were writing an essay. I always thought my teachers wanted me to sound like a robot or textbook. They'd use their red pen to cross out any originality. At university, I'd often try to use as many words as possible to reach the assigned word count. I'd write long sentences with many unnecessary words. Then I studied journalism, where writing succinctly – and as an unbiased observer – were keys to success. That helped me cut the flab from my writing, but I still needed to figure out *voice*.

The voice of each piece of writing should be different. My funny story for readers 7+ about training to be a fairy godmother should be noticeably different from my middle grade action-adventure book. However, our natural writing style is more difficult to change from piece to piece. I'm sure clever readers can spot my literary ticks and tricks in all of my books. For example, I love a dash and prefer shorter paragraphs. There's a way I tell a story. I can't completely change my background or personality. I try to lean into it and select stories that benefit from my style of writing.

Don't forget to play

Yes, practice is important but so is play. Sometimes we take ourselves and our writing so seriously. (Yes, I'm the queen of analysing absolutely everything.) And yes, writing is a serious business. But sometimes what we need is to relax and play more. If you are struggling with voice, take a break from your serious self and experiment with your story. Do what I like to call *off the page* writing. This is writing that might not find its way into the final draft of your story, but it might shake some ideas free. Write diary extracts from your protagonist at different ages, for example. Make a list of what she/he/they carry in their backpack or keep hidden under their bed. Write a monologue where the character introduces her/his/their self to a group of strangers. Get your character to write down their biggest fears or secrets. Put your character in funny, scary or outrageous situations and see what happens.

Excavating voice

Whether you've done so systematically or not, your story already has a voice. It's the unique way that you, and only you, can tell this specific story.

What would you say makes your writing unique? What impression have you created on the page?

To quote Sarah Davies again, she explained that voice is a combination of your experiences, personality, writerly skill, values, beliefs, interests, passions, fears and much more. All this feeds into the words you select, your syntax and sentence structure, and the literary devices you use. Every choice you make on the page combines to create the voice of your story.

It's worth repeating: you have a unique way of looking at the world. Your history and personality is like no one else's. We often think of the big personas – the people who grab attention the moment they walk in the room. Or the class clowns. Or the geniuses. But there are also the quiet voices that, if you listen, often share the truths of the universe. They might challenge you. They might draw you in to tell you a secret. Striving for truth and authenticity in your voice will give your writing the best chance of connecting with readers.

How do you know if you've managed to evoke an original and appropriate voice for your work? This is a tough one. I don't think there are any writers who finish a draft that they'd worked on for any amount of time and think, *It's a great book, but no voice.*

The next exercises will test the voice in your piece and offer some ideas if you think it isn't as good as it can be.

Exercise

Spotlight on you and your protagonist

In *Voice: The Secret Power of Great Writing*, James Scott Bell defines voice as the 'character's background and language filtered through the author's heart, and rendered with craft on the page'. The next exercises will break this down for your story.

My current work-in-progress has three main characters. It's told in a close-third person with each character taking turns sharing the story. I created a series of quick bullet points to help remind me of the unique voice I wanted for each character. Here's an example from Jada, one of my characters.

1. ***13 years old***. When writing for children and teens, it's always important to remember their age and maturity level. This shapes world view, logic, word choice, metaphors, etc.

2. ***Female***. It's my hope that gender won't matter as much to current and future generations. But in my experience, from the moment the doctor shares your gender with your parents, it influences how you are treated. Think about how a character's gender influences them. Consider whether your character identifies with the gender they were assigned at birth, how they express themselves, and how they feel about their gender.

3. ***An artist at heart***. She wouldn't claim this title for herself, but she sees the world through the eyes of an artist. She uses poetic descriptions, few complex sentences and sentence fragments when she's describing something or someone.

4. ***Quirky observations***. The connections her brain makes are unique and original. For example, she sees emotions as colours.

5. ***Negative self-talk***. She's critical of herself, always internally criticizing her actions and thoughts.

It's your turn. **What are five key aspects of your main character that will influence how she/he/they tell the story?**

1. _____

2. _____

3. _____

4. _____

5. _____

The second part of Bell's definition is about you. Do a similar exercise, but turn the spotlight on yourself.

Here are a few examples from me.

1. ***I'm an optimist***. I try to see the best in people. I try to make the best of any situation and when bad things happen, I try to learn from them and be a better person.

2. ***I'm originally from the United States***. I have that cheerleader nature that people have told me is very *American*. I'm down-to-earth, and as far from a literary snob as you can get.

3. ***I'm a planner***. I love a to-do list. I plot my stories before I write a word. I want my stories to have a strong pulse and page-turning pace.

4. ***I studied journalism***. I have a bachelor's degree in journalism and worked in public relations for 17 years. My natural inclination is brevity.

5. *I strive for accessible and relatable prose*. I want my writing to be accessible to any reader. I don't talk down but neither do I use words, phrases or sentence constructions that might alienate a reader.

6. *I find the humour*. In life and literature, a sense of humour is important. I try to add levity to my life and fiction.

Can you list a few things about you that influence your writing?

1. _____

2. _____

3. _____

4. _____

5. _____

The final part of Bell's definition has to do with your knowledge and skill with the craft of writing. This entire book is breaking down how you tell a story – and showing you how you might improve your draft. In Chapter 8, I offer a highlighting exercise, which might be helpful for you to uncover how you tell a story. But for now, answer these two simple – but challenging – questions.

How would you define your writing style? Or at least what is your aim? I have a casual, accessible writing style. Some writers strive for a literary style. Define yours.

What is the ideal writing style for your book? Consider the genre and ideal age range of your readers – everything you listed about the character. Take into account the setting and time period too!

EXERCISE IN ACTION

Earlier in this chapter, I shared the bullet points I created for Jada, one of the main characters in my middle grade work-in-progress, working title *The Day of the Protest*. The extract below is the opening chapter from Jada's point of view. I've annotated it to demonstrate how I crafted a unique voice for this piece.

Jada peers into her kaleidoscope. One eye open wide, the other wrinkled tightly shut. The colours dance in patterns creating order and chaos with every tiny twist of the end cap. Jada's vision is fuzzy from sleep. Yellow. Blue. Red. Primary colours merge into every shade of the rainbow. The pieces click softly as they tumble and fall into place, forming a momentary masterpiece.

Kaleidoscope is a metaphor for the theme of the book. How people can look at the same issue but focus on different aspects.

Jada is an artist at heart. Her close third person point of view has a more poetic feel. She often thinks in sentence fragments.

Underlined throughout the extract are places where I've used sensory detail, sharing Jada's impression of her world.

When her parents fight, Jada disappears into her kaleidoscope. A mirrored triangle in a toilet roll tube. Three coloured objects and a source of light to bring the colours to life. She searched for ages to find the items for her kaleidoscope. A fragment of sea-polished glass from her daily walk along the muddy bank of the Thames. A jewel retrieved from a crack in the floor board from a necklace Dad yanked from Mum's throat. The final item a cheap bead from

Each item in her kaleidoscope shows a part of her backstory.

a bracelet, a gift from a friend she had once in real life.

Her parents have been at it all night. It always starts the same. Low staccato voices seeping through the crumbling mortar between the bricks. At first it's only a hum of hushed voices. Back and forth like a duet. Jada can sleep through that. But it has escalated into words of one syllable.

'Idiot!'

'Arse!'

She twists the end cap slowly shifting the triangle pattern that repeats along the tube. She tries to focus on the colours and shapes. It's no use.

CRASH!

Jada sits bolt upright at the sound of breaking glass. Her parents should reconsider their household ban on plastic. She slips on her fluffy cream robe and matching slippers, paint-splattered. They envelop her in warmth from the cold, spring morning – and the icy chill of the fight.

They live in London's Docklands on the north shore of the Thames on the top floor of a converted warehouse. Sometimes she's sure she can smell the tea and tobacco that were stored here when kings beheaded people at the Tower of London a few kilometres away. The space is the size of her primary school hall, which she hasn't seen since the pandemic. Her parents used

Crumbling mortar
Hum of hushed voices
Back and forth like a duet
These are examples of word and phrasing choices to create a specific effect.
I hope you can feel the rhythm in the writing.

Then there's a abrupt change here intended to jar the reader in a similar way to the jolt Jada feels when she wakes to her parents' fight.

I might reconsider the line about the parent's ban on plastic. It illuminates something about her parents but does so with humour. I'm not sure that it's not out of place here.

This is an example of how small choices contribute to the overall voice of the piece. I could have written:
She slips on her paint-splattered fluffy cream robe and matching slippers.
OR
She slips on her fluffy cream robe and matching slippers, which are a hand-me-down from her mother (or from early morning paint classes with her parents).
I chose a more unusual sentence construction with the adjective at the end. This decision had to do with the rhythm of the sentence as well as making the detail an after thought and leaving the why open to interpretation.
This paragraph is exposition, locating the reader in time and space – London, post-pandemic. I wonder if this is the right place for this paragraph. It pauses the action.

a world disaster as the excuse to save her from that 'bourgeois, fascist institution'. And any real-life friends.

She shuffles to their studio and slides open the door. She stands in the opening. Clenched fists stiffen her arms. She will not look away.

Silent protest.

It's the only way Jada can make them stop.

Mum hurls a glass muddy with paint brushes and stale water at Dad's head. He ducks. It crashes against the brick wall, blowing glass and water and sending paintbrushes somersaulting through the air. One lands at Jada's feet. Bright pink caked on the bristles. She flicks a shard of glass from her cheek and wipes away a dot of wet, which she realises is blood. They are screaming, creating a whirlwind of sound around her. Their faces and bodies contort, more monster than parent. She used to practically float with pride that such talented artists' blood ran through her veins. But now the same thought terrifies her.

The early morning sun streams through the wall of crossword-puzzle windows, but the room feels dark. She loves this room with its high ceilings. Paint flecks layered like permanent fireworks across everyone and everything.

Another example of how sentence construction and brevity create a staccato feel to the writing.

The two words – silent protest – are important. I needed them to stand alone so the reader might linger a moment with them. It's the juxtaposition and contrast of these words that I want my reader to ponder. The power of silence as a protest.

I've tried to make this fight scene more visual and poetic so even in this moment of chaos, Jada still focuses on the beauty.

Canvases polka-dot the walls. Her dad's work a bold chaos of colour, inspired by Jackson Pollock. Her mum's equally colourful surrealist portraits, a homage to her hero Frida Kahlo. Jada's name a mash-up of both artists' first names.

These lines of exposition may need to be cut. I liked the origin of Jada's name, but again am I pausing the action for information that my reader doesn't need to know yet? Also my young readers might not know who these artist are. (My five-year-old granddaughter did recently tell me about Frida Kahlo.) Maybe that's okay, but maybe not in the opening pages. I haven't decided yet.

Her parents lunge for each other. Jada can't tell if they will embrace or attack. Mum's hand connects with Dad's cheek in a sharp crack. Dad grabs her wrist, mid-air. They glare daggers. Chests heaving.

That's when they notice Jada. Their limbs fall slack.

This is the climax of their fight. I've used short sentences to enhance the drama of the moment.

Exercise

Learn from your hero

Pick a fiction book you love, one you might quote from time to time. Ideally, this would be for the same age range and in the same genre as the book you are writing.

1. Find that special passage that speaks to you, the one you love.

2. Hand write it or type it out word for word.

3. Determine what about this passage makes it special for you.

4. Read it aloud. Find the rhythm of the passage.

What did you learn?

What could you apply to your work?

Exercise

Finding your voice

Select a paragraph or two from your novel, but no more than one page, that you think best represents the voice of your story. We all have those gorgeous moments in our novel of which we are most proud. Find yours!

STOP! Do not read on until you've selected the paragraph or page that you feel best represents your voice.

Did you pick the opening lines of your novel? If not, why not? We will spend time in a later chapter polishing your opening until it sparkles, but for now, all I'll say is that you must demonstrate the fresh, original and undeniable voice of your piece from the very beginning. If you picked another section of your novel, that's fine. I'd like you to do the following exercise for your opening page **and** the section you selected.

1. With pen in hand, read aloud the passage you selected. Circle where you stumble.

2. Put a line between each sentence.

3. Highlight nouns, verbs, adjectives and adverbs in different colours.

4. Put a box around any literary devices you use – metaphors, similes, imagery, symbolism, etc.

Now analyse your work.

1. Review the places where you stumbled when reading. This is often your subconscious telling you something's not working. Is it the rhythm or word choice? Figure out what it is. Revise until it rolls off your tongue.

2. Look at the structure, length and syntax of each sentence. Are your sentences simple, compound or complex? When and how do you use any type of clause? Do too many of your sentences start the same way: she did this, she said that, for example?

3. Look at your word choice. If you are writing in first person from the point of view of a 7 year-old, is each word appropriate for that character? Have you picked the perfect word for the experience you want to give readers, or is there a better word?

4. What literary devices do you use? Do you overuse them? Do they compete? If you have a wonderful metaphor, for example, don't clutter the paragraph with other devices that might detract from the one perfect one.

Sound, rhythm, sentence structure, word choice and literary devices are the ingredients that add up to the voice in your piece. Are you happy with what you've discovered? Have you identified where your writing may not be working to build the appropriate experience for your readers?

EXERCISE IN ACTION

Here's an example using the 'Finding your voice' exercise markup on page 145 from the opening of my novel *Half Lives*. We have used shading and underlining to indicate nouns, verb, adjectives and adverbs.

If you'd asked me that day whether I could lie, cheat, steal and kill, I would have said ab-so-lutely not. / I've told little white lies to my parents to stay out of trouble. / And, sure, I borrowed a few answers off Lola on that one chemistry test. / (Who cares that U stands for uranium or that it's number ninety-two on the Periodic Table of Elements?) / I shoplifted a Kit-Kat when I was seven on a dare, but I'd never kill. *Not possible.* I relocate spiders rather than squash them. / (And I hate those beasties!)

But now I've knowingly and wilfully committed all those acts on the Richter scale of freaking horrible – from lying to killing. / I'm not proud of it. I learned that surviving isn't all it's cracked up to be. / If you survive, you've got to live with the guilt, and that's more difficult than looking someone in the eye and pulling the trigger. / Trust me. I've done both. / Killing takes a twitch of the finger. / Absolution takes several lifetimes.

Note: I've not marked any literary devices because this piece doesn't have any. This is also a choice and literary style.

Enhancing your voice

If you are still struggling with voice, I highly recommend *Voice: The Secret Power of Great Writing* by James Scott Bell. It's one of the best books I've ever read on voice. It's only 115 pages long but is packed with some great exercises and insights.

Here are a few other tips to help you better understand voice and how you can enhance it in your work:

1. Review your responses to the exercise in 'Spotlight on you and your protagonist' on page 137. Can you rewrite a scene based on what you learned in this exercise?

2. Listen to an audiobook narrated by a voice you admire – and a voice that might be similar to the one you are trying to achieve. When I was writing an experimental project, I would listen to David Sedaris reading a few minutes from his essays before I'd start writing. I wanted the voice of my main character to have the same snark and funny insight as Sedaris in his essays. It really helped me get in the right mindset to start writing each morning.

3. Rewrite a passage of your book and take it to an extreme. If it's supposed to be scary, make it terrifying. If it's funny, how could you make it hysterical? If it's romantic, how can you make it passionate? Dare to be different. Don't worry about writing beautifully or even with perfect grammar. Experiment. The results might surprise you. Sometimes we are too careful with our prose.

Checklist

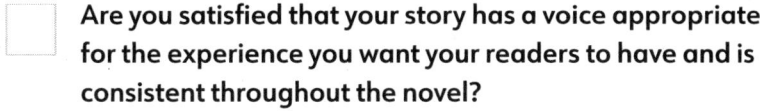

Are you satisfied that your story has a voice appropriate for the experience you want your readers to have and is consistent throughout the novel?

This is probably the most difficult aspect of your novel to improve because you already have a draft, and voice is your story's DNA, its essential ingredient. If you've decided that you need to enhance the voice of your piece, you must do the analytical work necessary to determine the right voice. This means understanding the structure, length and syntax you think is best for your story as well as looking at word choice and the literary devices you use. You must systematically edit your story on a nearly line-by-line basis to get the voice right.

Once you've found the right voice for your novel, make sure you maintain it from start to finish. One exception might be if your story is told in first person and your character significantly changes through the course of your story, in which case the voice of the piece might need to evolve. It's easy to start with a strong voice that unintentionally slips during the course of your draft. Also if the voice is too idiosyncratic, make sure it's not annoying or distracting the reader.

If you feel you need to construct a completely new voice – and you may want to sit down here, if you aren't seated already – it might be easier to work from the novel inventory you created in Chapter 4 and rewrite the book with a clear understanding of voice. Hear the voice in your head. Write a list of bulleted facts to keep in mind – age, gender, personality traits, quirks, vocabulary – that you review before writing. Find a trick to help you sustain the voice each time you write a new passage. For example, before each writing session, perhaps you listen to an audiobook or reread one passage of the book that captures the voice perfectly.

CHAPTER 7

Writing with authenticity

One of the most wonderful aspects of being a writer is that it allows you to inhabit characters of your own creation and imagine engaging stories. Whether you are questing for treasure in ancient faraway lands, galivanting through outer space, or creating a contemporary love story, research and attention to detail matter. But writing characters outside your personal experience demands special care – including sensitive interrogation of your motives and biases. This is true when:

- A character does not share your identity, including age, ethnicity, gender, sexuality, religion, class or disability, and especially if the character is from a marginalized group.

- Your story touches on any form of trauma you haven't experienced – for example, violence, racism, mental illness, life-changing accidents and illnesses, or care experience (such as fostered or adopted children or children in care).

Writing with integrity and authenticity is even more important when your readership is young. You are helping establish their world view. It's important that you don't unintentionally perpetuate stereotypes, misrepresent experiences, build bias, inadvertently 'other' or dehumanise people, or present outdated perspectives. You will need to consider how to sensitively and appropriately represent any difficult issues or ideas based on the age and emotional maturity of your readership.

Most of us – except those who are writing a memoir or something autobiographical – are reaching beyond our memory and into the realm of what if. In Chapter 2, I covered how to build three-dimensional characters. If you are writing outside your experience, you will need to do more – whether you're depicting your protagonist or a character in a larger ensemble. This chapter asks you questions and gives you broad areas to explore. I'll also point out the types of details you might want to double-check. But your examination doesn't stop there. You will need to find reviewers – often referred to as sensitivity readers, cultural consultants or authenticity advisors – who share the background of your characters. It's not enough to have a friend or family member give your story a second look. You need experts who will provide honest feedback – not only on the big picture, but on the minute details. You will need to invest in these critiques before you send your story to agents and editors. You owe it to yourself, to your readers and certainly to those from the communities your book represents.

How we talk about diversity/inclusivity/authenticity continues to evolve as all writers, regardless of background, are part of the ongoing dialogue. The terms and examples used are based on current UK norms and practices at the time I wrote the book. In the space of one chapter, I can't cover all the various ways people are unique, nor can I offer examples from every aspect of identity and experience. The issues surrounding inclusivity are important to me, readers and the publishing industry. I've sought advice from several experts in inclusivity. I'm sharing what I've learned, but I still feel I have more room for improvement. One reason I wanted to include this chapter is because it's information and advice I'd wish I'd known sooner in my career. There are marginalised secondary characters in my previous work that would have benefited from a more intensive interrogation. I will continue to educate myself – and I hope you will too.

Consult experts early on

Beth Cox, children's book inclusion consultant, encourages authors to consult with individuals who have the lived experience covered in their story at a book's development stage. This early consultation helps to authentically shape characters and action – and can inspire authors to be more creative. She recommends:

- Considering the character and plot you want to depict and what you need to know. Carry out in-depth research and find out as much as possible.

- Consulting people with the lived experience related to your character and plot (and make sure you pay them for their consultancy). Ask them to share insights and experiences to help you develop and add nuance to your character profile and story arc.

- Finding out more than you think you need to know and more than will make it into the final book.

- Checking back with those who helped you with research, and continue to question your biases, throughout your project development.

- Ensuring the editing process considers inclusion overall, and checking the tone, language and whether stereotypes have been perpetuated across all facets of diversity, not just those that are prominent in the story (sometimes known as an inclusion read or edit.)

Tough questions

You've purchased this book presumably because you have a first draft of a novel. If your story is from the perspective of marginalised characters or includes trauma that is not your own lived experience, my expectation is that you've already conducted extensive research and asked yourself many tough questions before you started writing, including *Why am I writing this story?* and *Is it my story to tell?* We can write stories for the right reasons and still do harm. If your story is outside your lived experience but important to you and you feel compelled to write it, you must be willing and able to thoroughly and thoughtfully review and revise your novel to the level of detail outlined in this chapter. If not, you should think carefully whether to continue developing your novel.

Some writers may not even be aware that they are including a traumatic experience in need of additional attention. Review the issues, topics, themes and events covered in your story – not just your main plot, but subplots and plot points as well. Trauma can develop from many experiences, including overt acts of racism, but also every day microaggressions, for example. You should also research and seek advice on any event that could trigger your reader. Even if you have experienced life events that are covered in your story, it can be helpful to seek advice from experts on these issues.

This chapter is not meant to be discouraging or provocative. We all want characters from a multitude of identities with varied perspectives to be represented in literature. I'm asking you to create authentic characters – a fundamental part of the writer's job in crafting any story. I am not advocating or encouraging the appropriation of others' stories. If your story includes identities outside your lived experience, I hope you've already spent time seeking to understand the complexities of cultural appropriation. There are many excellent articles and information available to help you understand the nuanced issues of appropriation, including who gets to write, who gets published and who can afford to write.

The aim of this chapter is to encourage you to examine your motives and your work on multiple levels. I've provided a few examples to illustrate the points in the next section. I've avoided giving examples when I felt that including them might be triggering, offensive or propagate stereotypes.

Dos and don'ts

DO interrogate yourself first before you turn the same intense spotlight on your story. Check for unconscious biases and how your background has shaped your perspective of those who differ from you. We can also hold bias about ourselves and those who are similar to us. Bias is difficult to understand and accept in ourselves. Sometimes we can't see it in ourselves and our writing. That's why I advocate working with an expert advisor who can support you in developing your characters, review your work, and flag problem areas so that you can address them.

DO make sure that any portrayal of a character or event that is outside your lived experience is well researched and thoughtful. Your heart may be in the right place. For example, you want an inclusive cast of characters or you want to shine a light on an important issue or underrepresented experience. But you may do harm if you haven't taken the time to thoroughly research and understand the complexities of the people and events you represent in your novel.

DO create realistic, original and authentic characters – but don't define any character by one thing. Make sure your characters are multi-dimensional. A character is more than her/his/their culture, economic status, sexual orientation, gender identity, religious affiliation, trauma, or condition, impairment or difference. Subtly weave details about characters' marginalized backgrounds and experiences into your stories, integrating this into their portrayal throughout the book. For example, don't simply tell us that a character is Muslim. Be aware and show us how religion may influence what they wear, when they worship and their family relationships.

DO represent the richness of any experience or culture. Don't rely on generic or stereotypic representation. Not every British person likes football, nor does every Indian person like Bollywood. Be specific with your setting and character history. There is no universal experience for each country or trait. For example, India is a subcontinent with hundreds of distinct cultures. Each culture has its own religious practices, languages, clothing, food, in-jokes and everything in-between. Where exactly your character lives or is from will affect that character in countless ways. Again, diligent research with people who have that lived experience will help you give your readers an original and authentic representation. If your story features marginalised characters or characters who have experienced trauma, don't only focus on challenges or barriers. Show the positive depth and breadth of their lives, not just the difficulties.

DO create a cast of characters that reflects the reality of your setting. For example, in a contemporary story set in Oxford, it would strain credulity if all characters were of the same ethnicity. On the other hand, there can be specific settings or circumstances where reflecting an imbalance is authentic. It's natural to worry about how to describe a character outside your experience, but that doesn't mean you should make your cast of characters homogenous. Instead do your research and speak to people to make sure that your representation is respectful and your mix of characters realistic and authentic.

DO read, watch and ask questions. Devour nonfiction books and documentaries from the perspective you are trying to write, but make sure these points of reference are from current voices and have been accurately researched. Don't rely on fiction, films or TV series as your primary research. They can provide a point of reference, but they may contain views or representations that are inaccurate or harmful. They can also perpetuate stereotypes and promote bias. In all your research, consider the source. Who is telling the story, and from what perspective? Many books, TV shows and films that were popular in the past – and even some current ones – promulgate views or representations that are now considered inaccurate or offensive.

DON'T think you can achieve inclusivity by simply including characters with a variety of skin tones, giving one a mobility challenge or making one gay. A diverse cast of characters can enrich your story, but make sure each casting choice is the right one, made for the right reason – not to tick the 'diversity box'. Avoid tokenism as this has the opposite effect of what you wish to achieve. Do your homework to make sure that each and every character has depth and your representation is honest and true.

DON'T make the white, male, heterosexual, cisgender, non-disabled, Eurocolonial experience the default. Many books assume characters will be interpreted as white unless expressly told or described otherwise. If you are describing one character's skin colour, find a way to share the ethnicities of all your key characters without falling back on stereotypes. There's often a tendency to use food metaphors to describe people of colour, like chocolate or olive skin. These should be avoided. Also describing cheeks reddening with embarrassment, being blue with cold or green with illness may not make sense with all skin tones. Similarly, don't reinforce the presumption that there's a gender binary and being cisgender and heterosexual are 'the norm'. Naturally include a range of gender expressions and identities without it being an issue or unusual.

DON'T trivialize trauma. Trauma can develop from many experiences. If your book touches on subjects that could be linked to trauma – including alcoholism, bullying, racism, a violent crime, exclusion or neglect, or care experiences – and you lack firsthand knowledge, tread carefully. If the book's main plot revolves around a trauma, you will need to do significant research. Even if the trauma is part of a subplot or secondary character's story, you will still need to invest time and energy in understanding and respectfully portraying characters who have lived through it. The orphaned child is an overused trope in children's fiction, which can be harmful. Losing a parent(s) and/or being adopted or being taken into care is a profound event in a child's life. Some stories rely on these tropes and often provide inauthentic and even harmful portrayals of children with these backgrounds. Be cautious about framing adoption or care experiences solely as trauma. These stories are complex and often include joy, resilience and growth. Over-simplifying risks perpetuating stereotypes.

DON'T think your imagination is enough. You will need to put in hard work, immersing yourself in whatever aspect of your novel is outside your experience. Interview people in the community you are representing. Get multiple perspectives of the same background. Research every aspect and every angle you can think of. This level of detail is necessary to enable you to develop and present authentic characters. The in-depth knowledge you gain in research will also allow you to be more creative with the character. However, don't impart all the research to the reader. Determine what information is necessary to include.

Think big, think small

Review big issues but don't forget the details. As I mentioned, it's not possible to cover in one chapter every aspect of every cultural, economic, sexual, religious, ethnic, gendered and disabled experience or trauma. I hope that the following list will open your eyes to the big and small ways you will need to review your novel. Think about how your own life experience and circumstances have shaped not only your world view but also your vocabulary and even your wardrobe. Getting the details right can have a big impact because they are what tend to reveal and build unconscious biases. This large- and smaller-scale thinking is necessary to ensure that your characters not only do no harm to the people and communities you are representing, but also offer readers an authentic and thought-provoking story.

- **Character world view** – Know the stereotypes and tropes associated with your character's experience of marginalisation – whether cultural, economic, sexual, religious, ethnic, gendered or disabled – and avoid them. Also express how a character will act or react based on their world view, not yours. For example, how a character might respond to an authority figure, such as a police officer or a politician, can vary significantly based on their background, age and lived experiences.

- **Plot and subplots** – In Chapter 3, you analysed your plot and subplots. List them again and determine if they might cause harm and if they are realistic for the character. Avoid playing into harmful tropes. For example, is a Black character there only to serve as a conduit to epiphany or understanding for your white characters? (There's even a term for this: the magical negro, which is a trope in American cinema, television and literature.) Do you have a fat* character who serves as a self-deprecating sidekick who will only be happy when she/he/they lose weight? Is a disabled character only there to offer inspiration? Is a bisexual or gay character the murder victim? Does a villain have a physical or facial difference, which is another common trope? These types of plot choices could be considered lazy and often send the wrong message.

- **Theme** – Review your theme again with a sensitive eye. If you don't think your story has a theme, think about what message your reader will take away. If your story was a fairytale or one of Aesop's Fables, what would the moral be? Make sure it's what you wanted your readers to learn and it's not damaging to the people and communities represented in your story. Gone, I hope, are the days of the damsel in distress who needs a man to save her or a disabled character who is magically cured by fresh air or other simple, nonmedical means.

- **Language** – Consider the words, phrases, and vernacular your character uses. Is the language appropriate for their background? Ask someone of the same background to review your dialogue to ensure it rings true. It's challenging to write in an accent if it's not your own. You will need to interrogate each sentence at a microscopic level to make sure you have every aspect of the accent correct. Also, be specific about where your character is from. Americans not only speak in a wide variety of regional accents, they also use different phrases and words to describe the same thing – the soda/pop/seltzer/soft drink conundrum. Every country has these types of regional differences.

---

* *Fat* – This one little word is a great example of not only why this chapter is important but the intensity of thought necessary when including triggering issues in your work. I hate the word *fat* and have ever since I was called fat for the first time at six years old. I used the term *overweight* in the first draft of this book. On the initial edit by the publisher, the editor suggested I changed *overweight* to *fat*. Well, I was insulted. I consulted an activist in the fat liberation movement so I could respond to my editor with an expert in my corner. However, the expert shared with me that the acceptable term was, indeed, fat. What? She explained that the term *overweight* implies a normative weight. Oh. The word fat is being reclaimed by this group underrepresented in fiction. Owning the word takes the power away from what was once considered insulting. Even though I dislike the word, I wanted to be correct, so I put it back in the draft. Then at the next phase of editing the book, a copyeditor crossed out the word and inserted the word *overweight* again. I explained that I had educated myself and shared the reasoning why the word was used. There's not one universal experience for any representation or trauma. I'm including this footnote because it's an example of seeking expert advice, listening and learning.

- **History** – It's not enough to look only at how things are today. Does the past influence your character – not only the personal backstory that you've imagined, but the broader history connected to that character's experience (i.e., ethnicity and religion)?

- **Physical appearance and mannerisms** – Signalling your character's ethnicity or disability, for example, with stereotypical traits can be offensive. Once you've pictured your characters, dig deeper. How would these traits influence their actions and mannerisms? It's easy to get the big picture right but the details wrong. For example, you may have done your research and described your Black British character's hair as curly or coily, not wild, kinky or frizzy, but then you might not have understood how to appropriately describe hair styles or you might have them running their fingers through their hair, which is a gesture that someone with this hair texture might not do. You might even need to consider genetics. For example, if you've written a disabled character, you need to know if the condition is inherited and how this might affect other members of the family.

- **Family** – Everything from how your character addresses another family member to her/his/their connection to and habitation with extended family may be culturally influenced. If family plays a role in your story, build a family tree and understand how your character has been shaped by her/his/their heritage. Also, there are many types of families, including same-sex parents, one-parent families, blended families, adoptive parents and children brought up in care, by a member of their extended family or a guardian. These family situations can be complex and will certainly influence your character. Writers may make these decisions about character background in a good-hearted attempt to be inclusive, but the representations can be shallow or harmful if not carefully and thoughtfully researched and represented.

- **Religion** – Often we never reveal or explore the religious beliefs of our characters. But if you have a character with a declared religion, make sure you understand its history, traditions, behaviours, morals, and practices. Don't portray any religion generically. It's impossible to know exactly how many religions exist globally, estimates range between 4,000 and 10,000 and within those can be a variety of traditions and denominations. For example, there are more than 45,000 Christian denominations globally, according to the Center for the Study of Global Christianity. Know specifically what your character believes and how that will influence every aspect of the character's life.

- **Gender** – What is your character's gender identity? How do they express this? Even if it's not shared in the book, knowing whether your character identifies with the gender they were assigned at birth, how they express themselves, and how they feel about their gender will add nuance to their representation. Also avoid falling into the stereotypical 'tomboy' or 'effeminate boy' tropes when representing gender.

- **Names** – Research your character's first and last names. Culturally names are a mixture of law, tradition, fads and family. Have you selected the right name based on these aspects of your character? Also don't assume a character's name is an accurate predictor of gender or ethnicity. You may need to find additional ways to respectfully share these aspects of your character.

- **Pronouns** – What pronouns do your characters use? How will you share this with your reader?

The list above isn't exhaustive. You'll need to do everything you can to create a story that accurately portrays the life experiences of your characters. And when you can think of no other way to review your novel, hire a sensitivity or authenticity advisor, more than one if you can, because there are multiple perspectives on any experience. The problem is that you don't know what you don't know. Professional sensitivity/authenticity advisors can help you fill gaps in your experience and correct any unintentional flaws. Listen to what your reviewers are saying. Hiring a sensitivity or authenticity advisor is not a tick-box exercise. You must listen, ask questions and revise your novel based on their recommendations and your discussion – and be prepared to make significant changes.

Checklist

☐ **Are you the right person to share this story, and if so, what are your motives for doing so?**

These questions can be uncomfortable. You will need to understand any bias you might have and make sure it's not found its way onto the page. Your heart can be in the right place, but think long and hard about whether you can authentically bring this story to life. This is the time when writers might set aside a story or do a lot more research to make sure they are appropriately representing any characters or issues that are not part of their personal experience.

☐ **Are your plots, subplots, themes and character portrayals authentic?**

How have you ensured authenticity? Who have you spoken to? Have you relied on stereotypes? It's important to do a deep examination of your story and characters. Hopefully you have done lots of research and spoken to those with lived experience. An authenticity advisor can help to identify anything problematic and suggest what you might need to do to authentically represent the people, cultures, religions, lifestyles, issues and trauma represented in your book.

☐ **Have you considered every word choice and detail and know that it positively and appropriately represents the people, communities and life experiences portrayed in your book?**

Your authenticity advisor may be able to help with this, but this is truly the level of detail and dedication necessary when writing a story that's outside your lived experience. The key is to listen and learn from the feedback, ask questions, and improve your novel based on what you've learned.

CHAPTER 8

Sentence by sentence

Only when you are happy with the shape and structure of your novel should you turn to this chapter for a detailed look at how to edit line by line. First, we will discover how you tell a story with my system of colour coding. This will help you understand the balance – or imbalance – of action, description, and dialogue in your manuscript. This will also help you weed out any unnecessary exposition. So grab some highlighters and your magnifying glass as we scrutinize every line.

I suggest you go old school and print out a clean copy of your manuscript and use coloured pens and highlighters for these exercises. This way you can spread out your novel and look for trends in your writing much easier than if you were reviewing it on your computer. You can use the same printed copy for most of the exercises in this chapter.

Every single sentence is important and should be necessary. When reading our own manuscripts, we read what we *thought* we wrote. These exercises will help you read what's actually on the page and determine if each line is essential to your story.

Exercise

Review sentence by sentence

All you need is a pen with a bright colour of ink. You can – as demonstrated below – use a backslash after every sentence if editing on your computer. However, it's not as easy to see the marks when we are trying to look at multiple pages. It's also a pain – once you've finished this exercise and made any changes – to go back and remove the backslashes. This is the most simple exercise in the entire book. All I want you to do is place a line between each sentence. That's it.

I've demonstrated using the opening of the first book in my *Magic Trix* series. Your manuscript should look like this.

/ The long black tail swished from side to side with each tick tock. / The yellow googly eyes looked left then right. / The big and little hands clicked into position, both pointing straight up. / Trixibelle's black cat clock meowed twelve times. /

/ It was midnight. / Trix's birthday was officially over. / She was ten years and one day old. / Double digits. That was nearly a teenager. / Like every year, she'd asked for a kitten. / She squeezed her eyes shut and wished and hoped and prayed one last time. / She crossed her fingers and toes and even whispered 'Abracadabra' for extra luck. /

I want you to spread out the marked-up pages of your novel one chapter at a time on a table or on the floor or use the multi-page view on your computer. Now analyse your prose sentence by sentence.

1. Look at the length of your sentences. If you are writing for 5–7 year-old readers, you won't want too many long sentences. It can put off new readers. Too many long sentences in a row can also confuse experienced readers. Make sure any long sentences are easy to read

and follow. If there's any confusion, consider breaking the longer sentence into two – or even three.

2. Does the length of sentences match what you are trying to achieve in this scene? Shorter, punchy sentences can make action scenes feel more breathless. Longer sentences can allow a reader to linger in a dramatic scene.

3. Review the construction of your sentences. Do you tend to overuse certain constructions? Prepositional phrases to start sentences? Gerunds after attributions? I find writers do this a lot: he said, shaking his head. She explained, rubbing her hands. He shouted, walking away. If you find this sort of repetition – a writerly tick – change up your writing. We don't want readers distracted by the author's style; we want them swept away by the story.

Discovering how you tell a story

As I was writing this section, I received a text from a writer who years ago took one of my workshops on revision. She sent a picture of her beautifully colour-coded work-in-progress. Her unsolicited text read: 'The colour coding technique from your workshop never fails. Trusty editing tool.' I hope you find it as useful.

Exercise

Colour-coded analysis

It's best to use the printed (or electronic) copy you used for the previous exercise. You will need four different colours of highlighters, but you can colour code using the highlight function on your word processing software.

Work through your manuscript line by line. I want you to highlight each of the following in a different colour:

Dialogue – This is speech that's separated by single or double quote marks, but I also mark any internal dialogue – characters thinking or speaking to themselves – with the same colour.

Action – Next, highlight in another colour any action. This can be dramatic action. *Mason leapt into his red Corvette and sped away.* Or small actions. *Evie wiped the sweat from her brow.* Or *Brooke winked.*

Description – Pick another colour highlighter and mark any description. This can be setting the scene, building atmosphere or describing a character.

I suggest highlighting dialogue first. It's the easiest to identify. You might find that some lines do double duty. Also some lines won't have any colour yet.

Exposition – The sections that are not highlighted are typically sections of exposition – places where you are telling your reader something.

EXERCISE IN ACTION

Here's an example where I've highlighted text from the first chapter of *Chasing Danger: Mystery at the Ice Hotel*:

Colour Key: Action   Description   Dialogue   Exposition

I slammed my back against the tree trunk and locked eyes with Mackenzie. She was crouched behind another tree a few feet away. Our breath puffed little clouds in the icy air. I slowly scanned our surroundings. No sign of them anywhere, but they were out there, waiting to attack.

Snowflakes fluttered down, blanketing the forest in silence. We had tracked them here, but they had zigzagged in the snow to mask their exact hiding spot.

What was that?

My body stiffened. The sound was no louder than the flutter of wings. Or was that the crunch of snow under tiptoe?

There it was again. Mackenzie'd heard it too.

We were sitting ducks if we stayed here. They were better trackers. They'd lived in this forest all their lives, running every inch of it. What chance did we have to outsmart them? But we had to try.

I gestured to Mackenzie that it was time to move. She nodded. My gloved hand counted down.

Three ... two ... one...

We bolted from hiding, lunging forward from tree to tree. The snow was more than a foot deep, and we struggled to move in our snowsuits and boots. The protective gear and our heavy breathing deadened our senses. We didn't hear them coming.

'AAAHHH!' Mackenzie screamed.

When you've highlighted three chapters, spread the pages on the floor and just look at the colours. What do you notice about the mix and quantity of colours? Do you see any patterns? Is this what you expected? Too much or too little of any colour?

What did you learn about the way you share a story?

What will you change? Anything you will adapt in the next revision and try to change in future stories?

Once you've completed the highlighting for the entire book, review your manuscript one colour at a time.

Dialogue – Note what each conversation is trying to achieve. What is the purpose of each section of dialogue? Is there too much dialogue? Too little? Can you cut to the heart of the conversation? If you transcribe a real conversation, you'll see it can be rambling and hard to follow. Dialogue in a book must have the illusion of authenticity, not the sprawling, random nature of most actual conversations.

Look at how you attribute each quote. *He said/she said* is the standard. For younger readers, you might want to attribute every line of dialogue. For longer exchanges of dialogue with little attribution, younger readers can lose track of who is speaking. It's okay to switch up attribution when it's appropriate – *She shouted. He explained* – but don't use too many distinctive attributions: hissed, stated, barked, etc. These can make your reader notice the attribution, not the dialogue. You can use actions before or after a line of dialogue to show who is speaking, but again if you use this too often, your readers will notice the writing.

Edit the dialogue based on what you've discovered.

Action – Do you have too much or too little action? Novels for children and teens should not be too passive. Maybe it's a reflection of how we see children in the real world, using computers, tablets or phones. If you are writing for children, you need ACTION. Something needs to happen. Yes, if you are writing a contemporary mystery, your characters would search the internet for answers, but it isn't exciting to read about someone reading and researching. Find appropriate ways to get your characters moving! Instead of learning something online, could they overhear a conversation or discover it by sneaking or spying?

At the opposite end of the spectrum, too much uninterrupted action can be exhausting for the reader. Make sure you give your readers some breaks, time to reflect and recover from intense action. If you are writing horror, for example, give your readers a moment of levity from time to time.

Read only the lines and sections that have action. Often writers will notice that they have actions that they use over and over – trembling hands, kissing teeth, or looking in a variety of forms (gazing, watching, examining, etc.) If you spot action that you repeat too often or too close together, correct this.

Also, this is a great time to review your characters' follow-through. If they sit down, have you noted when they stand up? If they close their eyes, have you informed your reader that they've opened them?

Edit the action based on what you've discovered.

Description – Review how you use description throughout your book. Do you consistently help your readers experience the setting and see your characters? In *Magic Trix*, my editor pointed out that I had an obsession with hairstyles. I described my cast of girlfriends initially by the style of hair – high or low ponytails, fringe, curly or straight. (I was a bit obsessed with hairstyles as a teen. During my last year in high school, I wore a different style every day of the week!) I needed to correct this in my story. However, if you have a character who dreams of being a hair stylist, commenting on hair would make perfect sense.

Do you have any ticks when it comes to description? There are no rules for how you weave description into your story. You do need it, but how much, when and why depend on the story. What atmosphere and style will suit it best? Do you always start with a description of the location at the beginning of a chapter? Do you ever point out what characters are wearing? Do you describe setting or character with three details each time or only one? Scrutinize how you use description and if it's giving your readers the experience you desire for your book.

Look at each description. Have you selected the right details to share with your reader? Are your descriptions working hard enough, creating atmosphere and revealing more about what your protagonist is thinking and feeling?

This might also be the time to look for changes of place, time or weather. Have you seamlessly shared these elements with your reader? Make sure your readers are aware of time passing and shifts in location. Weather enhances atmosphere but make sure it's consistently woven into the scene. If it's pouring with rain, do you have rain dripping from jackets? Puddles when the rain ends?

It's also a good opportunity to make sure you have place/time details right. If it's summer in London, it may still be light at 9 p.m., so your characters won't be hiding in the dark. I have a work-in-progress that's set in a seaside town. I created a tide chart for my entire story to check that the ebb and flow of my tide was represented consistently.

Edit the description based on what you've discovered.

Exposition – Sections of exposition can be necessary to move the book along or share something important with your reader. I opened my young adult novel *Half Lives* with a paragraph of exposition. (I included these opening paragraphs in Chapter 6 as an example for the exercise on voice.) The story was in first person, and my protagonist was telling readers what she'd learned throughout the course of the story they were about to read. It set the stage with a sense of mystery for what the readers were about to experience. Narrative summaries can help vary the rhythm and texture of story – but use exposition sparsely.

Many writers rely too heavily on exposition: they tell us too much. Renni Browne and Dave King said it best in their book *Self-Editing for Fiction Writers*; 'You don't want to give your readers information. You want to give them experiences.' Trust your reader and trust yourself as a writer. You don't need to tell us the characters are scared if you are showing us with shaking hands, heart pounding or sweat-dotted brow. Analyse every section of exposition and make sure it needs to be there. One exception: if your novel is for readers aged nine or younger, you may need to rely on exposition a bit more in order to connect the dots and explain more to your audience. They might not know that sweating is a sign of nervousness, for example. But if you are writing for middle grade and above, resist as much as you can the urge to explain.

Reduce, when possible, exposition throughout.

Exercise

Optional highlighting

Use this highlighting exercise to look at additional aspects of your storytelling, if you wish. You are limited only by the colour wheel and your budget for highlighters.

Flashbacks – I was once instructed by a creative writing tutor to eliminate all flashbacks. I'm rarely a fan of outright bans on any writerly device, but I do try to minimize the use of flashbacks – they interrupt the flow of a story and often give unnecessary information. If you are using too many of them, you may need to reconsider where you start your story or tell your story across multiple time periods.

Pick another colour highlighter and highlight lines or put a box around flashbacks. Look at where and how you use them. Try to avoid any flashbacks within a flashback (and yes, I've seen this more than once from my students). How close together are your flashbacks? This temporal back-and-forth can cause the literary version of whiplash. Is it necessary?

Background – I look at this when I'm writing anything other than contemporary fiction. Authors of dystopian, fantasy, and historical stories can be guilty of oversharing. We do loads of research and find out some amazing things about the time period when we are setting our story, and we want to show off what we know. Or we've created an unbelievably detailed world. We can't help but wedge in a few more details, right?

Select yet another colour and highlight lines or sections of background. You are looking for what I affectionately call 'info dumping'. These are large sections of background where you tell the reader usually about the world or the character. Cut down any large info dumps to only that which is essential. This is also the time when you can make sure any background or information you share is consistent throughout the story.

Background pushes pause on your story. Ask yourself my favourite question – *What do your readers need to know and when do they need to know it?* Does your reader need to know this background right here and right now – or at all? Don't interrupt exciting action or a poignant moment with background information, for example. If it's important, find another place to include it. We need enough background to show the reader they can trust us, that our research and our world-building is complete. Is there a way you can show this to your reader rather than tell them?

Exercise

Sentence-by-sentence edit

Once you've revised your novel based on the exercises in this chapter, it's time to read your novel sentence by sentence. Read each sentence and pause. Does it make sense? Does it follow on from the previous sentence? Is it saying something new and important? Did you stumble? Does it flow?

Don't give your reader a chance to look away. Elmore Leonard wrote in his manifesto, *10 Rules of Writing*: 'Try to leave out the part that readers tend to skip'. This can be large sections of information that we discussed in the previous section. It can also be passages of description or dialog that goes on too long. Are there moments in which you overly describe mundane details or actions? For example, *Evie stands up from her chair, walks across the room and switches off the light as she exits.* Your reader doesn't need every action. Some actions are implied. This sentence could be simplified to *Evie switched off the light as she left the room.*

To properly do this exercise will take a lot of time. When we read our novel for what could be the third or one hundredth time, we start reading every word, every line, but we become fatigued and unconsciously start to scan or speed read. We read what we think we wrote, mentally connecting the dots and filling in the gaps. To really read it properly, you must sit quietly and read aloud, one sentence at a time. Take lots of breaks. Maybe try to only do a few chapters each day.

I have done these exercises for an entire novel and found it very useful. My hope is that, like me, you experiment with the exercises in the book, learn from them and then apply what you've learned to any future books. After uncovering and analysing the instinctive way you write, you can adapt how you construct a scene. I do these exercises every so often to ensure I'm not falling back into old bad habits or acquiring new writerly ticks that I need to overcome.

Checklist

☐ **Do you understand at a sentence-by-sentence level how you tell a story?**

You have made sure that you've balanced action, description and dialogue in every scene. You have eliminated any unnecessary exposition and improved your sentence length and construction to maximize the readability of your prose.

☐ **Are you happy with each and every sentence?**

This seems obsessive, and it is! You have focused on every sentence and are happy that each and every one needs to be there, is well written and is in the right place.

CHAPTER 9

Word by word

We've moved from telescope to magnifying glass. Now it's time for the microscope. You will scrutinize every word on the page. Are your verbs working hard enough? Have you shared the right concrete details? Is the language you use appropriate for your character and the age of your reader? These exercises are easy to do, but they can give your prose a powerful punch.

Word choice

Now's a good time to double-check that your word choice is appropriate for the age, education and experience of your protagonist, if you are writing in first or a close-third person. Slush piles are littered with manuscripts featuring teen protagonists who thinly veil the adult author's voice and experience.

An additional hurdle for those of us who write for young readers: challenge but don't confound your readers. For the newest readers, you will want to consult an appropriate vocabulary list. If you are writing for more experienced readers, you can throw in a challenging word from time to time, but be cautious. If there are too many tough words, too close together, you might annoy or discourage your reader. Books for new readers should build confidence. We want the experience to be enjoyable so that we create readers for a lifetime.

Exercise

Word cloud

Use your favourite web browser and search for the words *word cloud*. Select one of the word-cloud generator sites. Cut and paste a copy of your entire novel into this site and, with a click of a button, it will generate a cloud of words that represents your story. Here's an example of a word cloud for my work-in-progress.

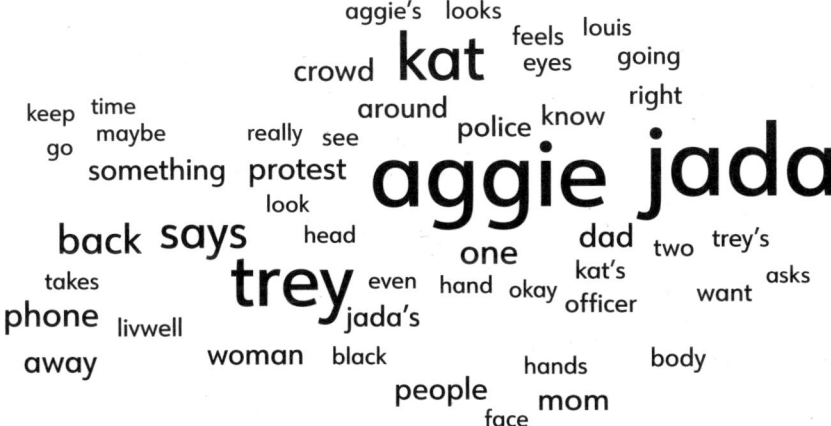

You can waste loads of time playing with the colour, shape and background. Don't! This is a serious diagnostic tool. (Okay, if you want to spend a bit of time making it pretty, printing it and framing it near your computer, go on! I'll wait here.) Either way, you'll have a visual representation of your story. Do you get a sense of your novel from the selected words?

Look at the size of the words. The biggest words are usually character names. Are these the characters you want to have the biggest presence in your novel? In my example, Aggie, Jada and Trey are my three main characters. They should be roughly the same size. Interestingly, Aggie and Jada are equal, but poor Trey is a bit diminished. I'll need to look at that. Kat, Mom, Dad and Louis also have significant roles but their sizes are appropriate for their importance in my novel.

You might want to check any other big words, for overuse. Use the *Find* function in your word processing software. When you type in the word in the dialogue box and hit *Enter*, it should show you the number of times the word is used in your manuscript and highlight that word in the text. There were a few surprises for me. I'd used the word *back* 99 times, *away* 92 times and *takes* 85 times in my 106-page manuscript. Yikes!

Review each time you use any of your overused words and see if every single one is necessary and the right word. Words like *back* can often be cut completely. Here's how I edited a few lines based on my overused words.

He points ~~her back~~ to her bedroom.
The discussion is **out of control** ~~getting away from her~~.
Dad ~~takes a~~ step**s** towards Jada.

Exercise

Powerful verbs

Ratcheting up your verb choice can add power to your prose. It's a simple exercise, but it can improve your story dramatically. A little test to see if your verbs are working hard enough: circle every verb on your first two pages. Then read them aloud – only the verbs, one after another. Do you get a sense of the action of your opening?

Here's an example from *Chasing Danger*. The verbs in my opening paragraphs are: shouted, waved, stand, survive, abandoned, felt and scream. Yep, I'm pretty happy with those. How about you? Are you happy with your verb choice? If so, that bodes well for the rest of your novel. If not, review your verb choice throughout your novel.

Wherever possible, eliminate any passive verbs – is, am, are, was, were, etc. – when they stand alone. *There's a black cat sauntering through my tulips.* Easily transforms into *A black cat saunters through my tulips.* Here's another: *Brooke has long blonde hair.* Nothing wrong with this statement, but it's also easy to eliminate this passive verb by combining with an active statement. *Brooke's long, blonde hair whipped in the sea breeze.* Also quickly fix those verbs where the subject of the sentence isn't performing the action. *Evie was bitten by a dog* becomes *A dog bit Evie.*

Look for lazy verbs – ones that aren't specific. *Get* is one of my lazy verbs. He gets into the car. She gets a drink. The phrasing in both cases is very bland and not working hard enough. Instead, try: *he climbs* into the car. *She pours* herself a drink. Also check for verbs that might feel generic, such as run and look. There's nothing wrong with these verb choices, but there might be one that describes the action better – raced, dashed, staggered, stumbled or gazed, glared, glanced or even eyeballed.

Also, be on the look-out for verbs and actions you overuse. Mine have been smile, grab and on, one particular manuscript, curl.

Exercise

Concrete nouns

Repeat the exercise on the previous page but for the nouns in your manuscript. Look for precise language on important details. Can you visualize the scene by reading only the nouns and their surrounding modifiers? Concrete nouns do more than show us the setting, character or object. They bring the scene and characters to life. For example, what is the villain's mode of transportation? A car doesn't reveal much about the character, but a red Lamborghini or a rusty blue truck changes how we see the villain.

Let's enhance a sentence from the previous section: *She pours herself a drink*. 'A drink' is too generic. What she drinks says a lot about her character. She pours herself a Diet Coke, some coconut water or a sneaky bourbon. Each of those reveals something about her character or mood.

However, be careful not to jam-pack a sentence with too many concrete details. A reader might get lost trying to visualize what you are describing. For example, *Her curly, jet black hair fell into her almond-shaped, emerald green eyes as she glimpsed Mt. Everest and its snow-covered peak in the blazing orange glow of the sunshine*. This layering of imagery pulls readers out of the story and makes them notice the writing. Select concrete details with precision. Determine which best set the scene. Your nouns should work as hard as your verbs.

Tighten your writing

Some writers are naturally succinct and may need to let their writing breathe. They haven't set the scene or shown us that moment-by-moment action. They need to expand their prose. That said, I always find that the writers most difficult to help are those who are prone to over-writing and don't recognize it. You can have the most amazing idea, characters and setting, but if agents or publishers see they'll need to edit your work at a word-by-word level, they will probably pass on your manuscript.

In one short chapter, I can't review every way in which your flabby manuscript might need to diet, but let me give you a few of the edits I routinely make when critiquing manuscripts. Review the list, and then scour your manuscript and tighten your prose.

- Adverbs are relatively painless cuts. In his book *On Writing*, Stephen King actually calls for the elimination of adverbs. (He goes as far as to say, 'I believe the road to hell is paved with adverbs.') I agree that adverbs are usually unnecessary, but I wouldn't go so far as to call for an all-out ban. Very rarely (see what I did there?) are words such as *really, always*, and *very* needed. One place they often sneak in is when attributing a quote. *She said convincingly*. What does this mean exactly? Did she shout and fold her arms across her chest? Did she nod until her listeners' heads were bobbing in agreement? The context of the quote and the verb used as attribution are usually sufficient.

- Check for unnecessary phrases. A few of my favourite examples: his heart thumped ~~in his chest~~, he nodded ~~his head~~, she imagined ~~in her mind~~, he blinked ~~his eyes~~, ~~actual~~ facts, and at this moment ~~in time~~.

- I search my manuscript for the words *start* and *begin*. They aren't often needed. Is she/he/they really starting to do something or are they doing it? Similarly *seem to* and *appeared to* often can be eliminated. Do the clouds seem to part or do they part?

- Look out for repetitive, redundant description: cold, icy lips; my heart is numb, has no feeling.

- Minimize the use of the word *now, suddenly* and *and then*. They're often unnecessary because the second described action generally follows the first directly.

- And the final one I'll share is getting down to the micro level. Remove any unnecessary qualifiers, such as head ~~off~~, stand ~~up~~, meet ~~up~~, sat ~~down~~.

Filtering

One easy way to tighten your writing is to remove any *filtering* in your manuscript. This will not only cut your word count but also make your prose more powerful. Filters separate your readers from the action, weakening your prose. Here's an example of writing that includes the layer of filtering:

The plane's wake **seemed to** rock the dock. I **felt** myself being catapulted into the air. I **knew** there was absolutely nothing I could do. I screamed as I plunged butt-first into the ocean. Big mistake. I **realized** the sound was strangled by gallons of water splashing over me.

I **wondered** what my dad would do. What had he told me NEVER to do in an emergency? Oh, yeah – panic.

Too late.

I **felt** my lungs burning for air. I **saw** my short, pathetic life flash before my eyes, but maybe that was only a school of fish because my life wasn't that colourful. I needed to calm down, which wasn't easy when you lacked oxygen and were waging an epic battle with the Indian Ocean.

I **felt** myself claw my way to the surface and gulped in air. Two strokes and I was back at the dock.

Notice how the bold words filter everything through the narrator's experience and separate you as the reader from what's really happening. Here's the same passage, with the filtering removed:

The plane's wake rocked the dock. I was catapulted into the air. There was absolutely nothing I could do. I screamed as I plunged butt-first into the ocean. Big mistake. The sound was strangled by gallons of water splashing over me.

What had my dad told me NEVER to do in an emergency? Oh, yeah – panic.

Too late.

My lungs burned for air. My short, pathetic life flashed before my eyes, but maybe that was only a school of fish because my life wasn't that colourful. I needed to calm down, which wasn't easy when you lacked oxygen and were waging an epic battle with the Indian Ocean.

I clawed my way to the surface and gulped in air. Two strokes and I was back at the dock.

To search for filtering in your manuscript, look for these words: see, hear, think, touch, wonder, seem, decide, know, feel, notice, realise, watch, sound. Sometimes filtering is necessary; certainly, you should not cut all uses of the words above. But evaluate them each time you use them and make sure you're not creating an unnecessary wall between the reader and the experience.

Exercise

Cut and cut again

This is a quick test to see how much you need to tighten your writing. Pick two pages at random. Cut 100 words from these pages. You can cut one word at a time or remove paragraphs, but you must cut a 100 words in total.

Stop and cut the words before you continue with the rest of the exercise.

Find a trusted writer friend who is also a good editor. Ask them to review your edited two pages and cut another 50 words. When they are finished, have a discussion about what they cut and why. How easy was it for you and for your writer colleague to cut words from your manuscript? If you or your colleague easily condensed your prose and nothing was lost, that's a signal for you to repeat this exercise for your entire manuscript. Don't set a specific number of words per page, but try to cut wherever you can.

Checklist

There are only two things to check in this section – but they are big.

☐ **Are you happy with every word and its placement?**

☐ **Is every word appropriate for your character and your readers?**

Your verbs are powerful, your nouns and their modifiers concrete. You've eliminated overused and unnecessary words and tightened your writing as much as you can.

CHAPTER 10

Beginnings and endings

Once you're satisfied with the overall shape and minute detail of your novel, let's make sure you've done all you can to hook readers into your story and leave them satisfied. We will start by reviewing how you start and end each chapter to compel the reader to the last page. Then we'll focus on your opening chapters to make sure they are enticing readers into your story. What is the promised journey of the book? Finally, we'll consider the last chapters. Does the story fulfil that promise?

Exercise

Enticing readers to read on

Here are two quick-ish exercises to examine how you start and end chapters. You want to draw your reader into the next chapter. It's that 1 a.m. moment when you finish reading a chapter and think, I'll just read one more. At the end of the next chapter, you realise you can't leave the characters here. You'll never sleep wondering what happens next. On and on it goes. The next morning you wake up bleary-eyed but satisfied because you've finished the book.

I'm not encouraging sleep deprivation, but I want to make it difficult for readers to put down your book. Let's see how you manage this.

Read the final paragraph or two of each chapter, one after the other. Look at how you end chapters. Many writers consciously or unconsciously end chapters a particular way. Maybe you like to entice readers with a thought-provoking question or statement: How would Mason ever survive? Or you end with a line of dialogue.

I read an award-winning novel, which really was outstanding. However, the author ended several chapters with a phrase akin to 'if I'd only known then what I know now.' It was a serious book, but each time a chapter ended with a version of that familiar phrase, it made me smile. Noticing the writer's tick, I was being pulled out of a really great novel.

Some authors routinely end a chapter when the problem/crisis/conflict in that chapter has been resolved. If you do this, you may want to end a few chapters in the middle of an exciting moment. Leave your reader begging to know how the conflict you've created will ever be resolved. Make them turn the page and start the next chapter to find out. It's a popular tactic used by TV shows to make me binge the next episode.

If you find that your chapter endings are too similar. Switch it up a bit. Unless you are writing something like R.L. Stine's *Goosebumps*, a cliffhanger at the end of every chapter can be annoying; so can a question or an emotional statement.

Now do the same for the opening few paragraphs of each chapter. Read the start of each chapter, one after the other. (You can skip your first chapter. In the next section, we will focus on how you start your novel.) How do you hook the reader into a chapter? How do you orient them? Again, some writers have a habit of orienting readers first – the next day, twenty minutes later, etc. Orientation is important, but it's not typically what draws readers in and keeps them turning pages into the wee hours.

When I did this exercise for one of my novels, I realised I had started a few chapters in a similar, somewhat baffling way. I started in the middle of the action – which is good – but sort of flashbacked a few paragraphs later to orient the reader. I know. It sounds confusing even trying to explain it. To do it once might (might!) have made sense, but why I thought this technique of confusing chronology was a good way to open a chapter is beyond my logical revision brain.

When we isolate the start and end of each chapter, we recognize patterns that we might not pick up on when we read our books from start to finish. Finesse the first and final lines of each chapter to be distinctive – and defy me to put your book down.

Hooking readers from the opening pages

From the first few lines of your novel, you are creating a contract with your readers. You are demonstrating the type of story they are about to read. You are setting their expectations. I always think of it as starting a journey. What journey will you take your readers on? If I picked up your novel without knowing anything, I should have a sense of the journey I'm about to undertake by only reading the first page.

I've read a lot of opening pages. Not only as an avid reader but also as a writer, editor, lecturer and mentor. I've read more than 1,000 opening pages for the past nine *Undiscovered Voices* anthologies. I can tell from the opening paragraphs whether the extract will be a contender for the anthology or my reading pile. I call it *confidence on the page*. I can see immediately if I am in capable hands.

You should analyse your entire story before you finalise those all-important opening lines. Sometimes the opening lines are the last piece of the puzzle to fall into place. Let's look at a few cracking starts to novels. In one or two sentences, these writers managed to capture my attention and demand that I read on.

- 'It was a dark, blustery afternoon in spring, and the city of London was chasing a small mining town across the dried-out bed of the old North Sea.' – *Mortal Engines* by Philip Reeve (Scholastic, 2001)

- 'By the time Jazz got to the field outside town, yellow police tape was everywhere, strung from stake to stake in sort of a drunken, off-kilter hexagon.' *I Hunt Killers* by Barry Lyga (Little, Brown and Company, 2012)

- 'So, before we get into this, there's one important thing I should tell you – I've been to the end of the rainbow.' *The Secret Sunshine Project* by Benjamin Dean (Simon & Schuster, 2022)

- 'The first thing you find out when yer dog learns to talk is that dogs don't got nothing much to say.' *The Knife of Never Letting Go* by Patrick Ness (Walker Books, 2008)

- 'One minute the teacher was talking about the Civil War. And the next minute he was gone.' *Gone* by Michael Grant (Egmont, 2009)

- 'When my brother Fish turned thirteen, we moved to the deepest part of inland because of the hurricane and, of course, the fact he caused it.' *Savvy* by Ingrid Law (Puffin, 2008)

- 'We went to the moon to have fun, but the moon turned out to completely suck.' *Feed* by M.T. Anderson (Walker Books, 2003)

- 'The best day of my life happened when I was five and almost died at Disney World.' *Going Bovine* by Libba Bray (Delacorte Press, 2009)

- 'After all the times she had insisted that something was out there, after all the times no one believed her, after the lifetime of sniggering she had endured – tonight, Lucy Sladan would prove she was right.' *The Bigwoof Conspiracy* by Dashe Roberts (Nosy Crow, 2020)

This sort of gut-punch style of opening lines isn't right for every novel. Jennifer Donnelly opens *A Gathering Light* with the most poignant description of summer at the Glenmore Hotel on Big Moose Lake in 1906. The final line on the opening page, draws you beautifully into the story: *For I am good at telling myself lies*. You need to set the appropriate tone for your novel in your opening paragraphs. Set readers' expectations from the very start.

Exercise

First impressions

First impressions matter – in life and in a book. Read the opening page of your novel. Read it out loud and really focus on it. You've read it many times, I'm sure, but try to read it with fresh eyes. You are in a bookshop and you've picked up your novel. (Yes, visualise this moment. Won't it be amazing?!) Now crack open the book and read those opening lines. Try to imagine what your readers might expect from reading your first page.

What is the first impression you give readers about the novel they are about to read?

Great opening lines have four elements:

1. **A unique voice** – It's that elusive quality that every agent and editor look for. It's the original writing style that will bring your story to life. I need to hear and feel that spark in your opening lines.

2. **An intriguing hook** – How do you entice me to read on? You don't do that by telling me information. You do that by giving me just enough story to whet my appetite. You show me how your book is different from the thousands of others on bookshop shelves.

3. **Compelling character(s)** – Ideally, I want to meet the main character on your opening page. I should be intrigued by your protagonist. I don't have to like that person, but I should be excited to learn what she/he/they will do next.

4. **And a hint of the journey to come** – Can I tell in your opening lines if I'm reading science fiction, fantasy, romance, action, mystery or comedy? Do your opening lines reflect the tone and genre of the rest of the book? They should.

Here are a few other ways to capture your reader:

- Does your main character have a strong, idiosyncratic voice? As Ness does in the opening lines of *The Knife of Never Letting Go*.

- Set up your conflict or issue from the opening pages. Dean intrigues us with telling us he's seen the end of the rainbow while Grant shocks us with a disappearing teacher.

- Some openings start with a wonderful description; others thrust you into the action, as Roberts does in *The Bigwoof Conspiracy*. You may want to start in a scene with a character and a challenge. Start in the middle of the action and make your reader want to know what's happening and what will happen next.

- Does your story have an unusual setting or subject? The moon? Taxidermy? Lead with it, as Anderson does in *Feed* and Reeve does in *Mortal Engines*.

- Surprise the reader in some way. Bray does this with humour in *Going Bovine*, and Law does it in *Savvy* by telling us her brother caused a hurricane.

- Give the reader a sense of intimacy. Think of zooming in on one detail like Lyga does by opening with a crime scene in *I Hunt Killers*. Is there a compelling image that could start your story?

- Engage your reader with concrete images and powerful, precise language.

It's important to ask this of your opening: *What do your readers need to know and when do they need to know it?* As the writer, we know too much. We've developed a comprehensive backstory for our characters. We've done our research and unearthed scores of amazing tidbits that we are absolutely dying to share. Resist this urge. Entice your reader. Sprinkle in only what readers need to know. What you withhold from readers is as important as what you share.

EXERCISE IN ACTION

Below I've shared the evolution of the opening paragraphs of *Chasing Danger* – from the first sample to the final published work. I've explained my thought process and how the opening to this series was crafted.

Chasing Danger, Feb 2015
When this was written, I had a detailed storyline, but this was my first attempt at the opening paragraphs.

This vacation was going to be murder. Through the seaplane window, the sky and ocean merged creating an unnatural blanket of blue below me. It almost hurt to look at the sun reflecting off the water, creating what appeared to be a mix of liquid diamonds and the colour of a Blue Blast Mega gumball. The sun felt closer here. The heat seemed to reverberate through the twenty-seater plane. My body was coated with sweat as if my insides were being steamed.

> This was my attempt at a *killer* opening line. It sets the tone and offers a hint of the journey to come.
>
> This draft started with Chase on the plane approaching the island where the story would take place.
>
> Two phrases (underlined) that are nearly the same so close to each other might make my reader notice the writing.
>
> Although this opening paragraph has atmosphere, the descriptions are clunky. Two, longish, visual descriptions so close together – liquid diamonds and the colour of a gumball – might cause the reader to pause to try and imagine this. Eventually you'll see that I thought picking the best one had more impact.

For anyone over eighteen, this might be their idea of paradise. But the little dot of an island up ahead was going to be my home for the next month and it boasted – BOASTED – no Wifi, TVs or phones. Again if you were the kind of girl who could tan and liked spending endless hours doing nothing, then this was heaven. But

> This is exposition. It's telling my reader information, but not the most compelling start to this story.
>
> Chase's voice is starting to percolate here, and we are getting a sense of who she is, but everything is feeling a bit forced.

if your pasty white skin burned in ten minutes and your life revolved around a black screen of some dimension then this would be a modern re-telling of Dante's *Inferno*.

Although as an adult reader I like this reference, I ultimately realised that this wasn't a reference my readers would understand. I'm happy to challenge readers with new references and words, but I try to avoid it in the opening pages. I don't want anything to pull them out of the story.

Chasing Danger, May 2015
I'm still revising the opening before I sent it to my publisher.

This vacation was going to kill me. I was stranded on a twelve-by-twelve floating dock in the middle of the Indian Ocean. I had survived twenty hours trapped on a plane – forty-five minutes of that on a seaplane. My brain and mouth felt fuzzy from recycled air and plastic plane food. The seaplane pilot had ditched me and my duffle here before taking off with a roar and spray of salty sea. The dock rocked nearly tilting me off.

I still wanted that opening line hook, but realised that *kill* more accurately reflected the story. Chase is almost killed in the book – several times! However, this line feels wedged in.

Because my setting was unique – definitely a hook, I orient my readers early in my opening.

The sky and ocean merged into an unnatural blanket of blue around me. The sun reflected off the water, creating ripples of liquid diamonds. Its ray singed my skin like thousands of searing hot needles. Maybe it was my imagination, but after only five minutes of waiting, my pasty white skin appeared a shade pinker.

I've improved the description and atmosphere from my first attempt at an opening.

Chasing Danger, July 2015

This was the opening of the first complete draft I sent to my editor at Scholastic.

"Don't leave me here!" I shouted and waved wildly at the seaplane as it floated away with a roar and spray of salty water.

I was standing on a twelve-by-twelve floating dock in the middle of the Indian Ocean. I had survived twenty hours trapped on planes – forty-five minutes of that on a seaplane. My brain and mouth felt fuzzy from recycled air and plastic plane food. The pilot had tossed my bags on the dock and sort of shoved me out. If that plane took off, there was no turning back. Panic punched me in the gut.

I changed my mind. I didn't want to do this. "Come back!" I screamed as the plane cut a wide arc in the water, preparing to take off.

I decided the hooky opening line didn't work. I needed to start my action-adventure story with action. I start in the middle of a scene already in progress to intrigue the reader.

I orient my reader quickly here. The character is starting to come alive a bit more with details like *fuzzy from recycled air and plastic plane food.*

Chasing Danger, Sept 2015

This is from the second draft I sent to my publisher. Even though, the editor liked the opening paragraphs, I still finessed them a bit.

"Don't leave me here!" I shouted and waved wildly at the seaplane as it floated away with a roar and spray of salty water.

I was standing on a twelve-by-twelve floating dock in the middle of the Indian Ocean. I had survived twenty hours trapped on planes – forty-five minutes of that on a seaplane. My brain and mouth felt fuzzy from recycled air and plastic plane food. The pilot had tossed my bags on the dock and sort of shoved me out.

"Come back!" I screamed as the plane cut a wide arc in the water, preparing for take-off. If that plane left, I would be stuck here. There was nowhere to run, nowhere to hide. Panic punched me in the gut.

I deleted the first two sentences previously in this paragraph because my editor thought it was confusing. It wasn't clear what the main character had changed her mind about.
I upped the peril here and heighted my character's panic.

Chasing Danger, Final, Published Draft

"Don't leave me here!" I shouted and waved wildly at the seaplane as it floated away with a roar and spray of salty water.

I was standing on a twelve-by-twelve floating dock in the middle of the Indian Ocean. I had survived twenty hours trapped on planes – forty-five minutes of that on a seaplane – and then me and my bags had been abandoned here. My brain and mouth felt fuzzy from recycled air and plastic plane food.

"Come back!" I screamed as the plane cut a wide arc in the water, preparing to take-off again. If it left, I would be stuck here. Nowhere to run. Nowhere to hide. Panic punched me in the gut.

Based on notes from the copyeditor, I re-organized the paragraph for a bit more clarity. But otherwise the copy was the same as the previous version.

The final draft is punchier, shorter sentences with less exposition. The first version started as the seaplane landed, but this was ramping up. I needed to start with action.

Does my opening meet the criteria outlined in this chapter?

1. Unique voice? It's starting to spark on the page. I might have done a bit more to enhance the voice in the opening lines if I was writing this now, but I only mean a phrase or two. By the next paragraphs in the book, the character is really coming alive.

2. Intriguing hook? Starting in the middle of the action and with such a unique setting, I hope I've enticed the reader to keep reading.

3. Compelling character? You get the sense that she's a girl of action and the reader is hopefully feeling the peril of her predicament.

4. Hint of the journey to come? Yes, I hope readers can already feel the lure of the action and adventure to come.

Exercise

Test your opening

Once you've polished your opening, give the first two pages to a few writer friends or critique partners. I suggest asking three or more people, so that you can get a consensus. Ideally, these are people who have not read the book before and know nothing about it.

I prefer to ask writer and editor types because they usually have the language, confidence and honesty to respond to these questions. When I've asked friends and family, I have to spend time educating them on genre or age ranges in children's lit. Also, because they care about me, they won't want to offend or upset me so they often aren't as honest as they could be. What they forget is that as a writer who has been traditionally published, I've grown a very thick skin. Internally I might be cringing or crying when they give me their feedback, but externally I've mastered my aw-thanks smile and memorised my gracious next line: *thanks for your thoughtful and helpful feedback.*

If you don't have any writer friends, attending writing workshops and conferences can be a place to discover like-minded writers. The Society of Children's Book Writers and Illustrators (SCBWI) is an international organization with many local writing communities. They also have online critique groups. You can find your local SCBWI by visiting www.scbwi.org and clicking on the *Global Regional Chapters* section.

Here's the list of questions to ask once your selected critique partners have read your first two pages:

1. What is the genre and age group of this story?

2. Who is the main character?

3. What do you know about the main character?

4. What do you know about the setting?

5. What is the promised journey of this book? Beyond genre, what will the story be about?

6. Did you have any questions about the story?

7. What's the hook? What's unique or most unusual about the story?

Review all their responses together. You might have one critique that's an outlier. In my experience asking my students and workshop attendees to do a version of this exercise, there's usually some sort of consensus. Are you happy with what they've discovered? Don't argue with anyone who is critiquing your work. If it's not on the page, it's not on the page. Do ask respectful follow-up questions, though: Why did they think it was a fantasy or comedy, when you are writing a serious whodunnit?

Stop and revise the opening of your novel based on what you've discovered.

If you want to study great openings, download some of the past *Undiscovered Voices* anthologies. These openings were selected by an expert panel of judges from hundreds of submissions. The selected writers know how to hook a reader. Analyse why they worked and determine how you can apply this to your work. You can download the past anthologies for free at www.undiscoveredvoices.com.

The end

I'm going to be controversial here. (At least my husband thinks so.) Unless I am satisfied with the ending of a book, my review will be less than favourable. Your book can sing with voice and/or whip me into a reading frenzy with its fast-paced, clever twists and page-turnability. However, if the ending isn't satisfying – and I don't necessarily mean happy – I won't recommend it. A writer can pen an action-packed and emotional book that compels me to turn page after page, but the true mark of a genius is to create an ending that is inevitable, surprising and satisfying.

We often rush the endings of early drafts. The finish line is in sight, and we sprint before we collapse with exhaustion at doing that most extraordinary thing – finishing a draft of a novel. Often the final chapters get shorter and the writing more sparse because we are rushing. If this is the case, I hope you corrected it after you did your novel inventory in Chapter 4. Now we need to make sure you end your story with as much verve and care as you started it.

We discussed controlling idea in Chapter 3 – the moral of your novel. Are you still satisfied with how you leave your readers and what they will take away from your novel?

Most of us write and rewrite and polish and agonize over the opening chapters. Have you given as much attention to your final chapters?

Stop and read the final few chapters of your book.

Often, when giving our manuscripts the final read, we sit and read from start to finish. By the end we are exhausted and rushing – even if it takes us a few days to read the book completely. Take a moment to examine your final chapters independent of the rest of your novel. Read it aloud and really focus on what you are reading.

Now answer a few questions about your ending:

1. Does the climax of your story – the resolution of the main conflict – happen on the page?

Writing the ending is *huge*. Some writers write the ending early in the process. I outline my stories, so I know how I want the book to end, but I usually write my novels in order. I asked you early on: what does your main character want? Your climax is the moment we learn whether she/he/they get it or not. It's not uncommon for writers to shy away from the big moment. They've built it up and made it almost impossible to write. Instead of writing the *big* scene, they sidestep and tell us the aftermath. Not good enough. Only once or twice did I understand why a writer avoided committing the climactic scene to the page. It was because a twist was coming; had I seen the scene, the twist would have been ruined. Even so, I still felt a bit robbed because I didn't get to share that important moment with the main character.

2. Does it include the characters that are most important?

This is straightforward: who is in that climactic scene, and are they the most important characters?

3. Does it resolve the main conflict of the story?

Again, pretty clear cut. If it's a mystery, do I know whodunnit? If it's a quest, does the main character complete it? If it's a romance, do the main character and the object of her/his/their affection end the book together? Sounds like common sense, but sometimes writers don't resolve the main conflict. If you haven't, why not? And if not, will your ending still be satisfying?

4. How many pages or chapters after the climax do you end your book?

Don't hang about after the climax. End as quickly as possible after resolving your plots and subplots – to the extent you intend to resolve them. I've read several books recently where I felt the book ended and ended and ended. By the final page I was a bit fed up. About fifty pages after the main conflict of the story was resolved, the writer insisted on wrapping up everything neatly and telling me more than I thought necessary.

Also avoid an info dump at the end. If, like me, you love a little Agatha Christie, we have been conditioned to expect the denouement – that final scene in which all of the characters are gathered and the strands of the main plot are explained and resolved. The detective names each character and reveals why and how they could have done it, dismissing each character one by one until finally the last character is unmasked as the killer. While I sort of love this in old-school mysteries, it's nostalgic and may not be the best ending for your story.

Try not to have page after page in which things are explained to the readers. If you can, reveal things over the course of a few scenes and have the final ah-ha or big climactic moment that brings everything together.

5. How does the ending make you feel? How do you want readers to feel? Why does it work?

I love this quote by American writer and editor Gordon Lish: 'It's not about what happens to people on the page; it's about what happens to a reader in his heart and mind.' Have you written a climax that will satisfy my heart and head? If not, why not? How can you give your readers the appropriate emotional experience at the end of your book?

Inevitable, surprising and satisfying

Let's examine those three words that describe the best novel endings – inevitable, surprising and satisfying. It may at first seem contradictory to say an ending is inevitable *and* surprising, but I love when an author has crafted my experience so well that when the final piece of the story puzzle is placed, I say not only *ah-ha!* but *of course!*

The ending must also be satisfying. You can leave me in tears or angry at the injustice of life or content as the main characters ride off into the sunset – but don't disappoint me. You set up expectations in your opening chapter. Does your ending meet those expectations? It's okay to shock or end abruptly, exiting quickly after the climax. But are your readers getting the ending they deserve?

For younger readers, your ending must be relatively neat and tidy. Don't leave young readers with an unresolved ending or be too subtle and ask readers to connect too many dots. I'd also suggest that you have a happy-ish ending for young readers. Yes, be authentic and true with your story, but be kind to your young readers. If you are writing for young adults – all bets are off. They can take an unhappy or open-ended finale.

I hesitate to give examples because I don't want to spoil the endings of any books you might not have read. *Holes* by Louis Sachar is the best example of an inevitable, surprising and satisfying ending. Everything – every detail and moment – comes together perfectly in its final pages. Read it and you will see what I mean.

Think about the last impression you leave with your readers. Do the last line and the last visual pack an appropriate punch? Am I going to want to linger on them for just a moment more with a satisfied sigh before I close the book for good? That's what we all should aim for!

Exercise

The beginning and the end

Read the opening few chapters and read the final few chapters in one sitting. I'd say read as many chapters as necessary to reach the inciting incident of your book. As for the ending, start with the chapter that includes the climactic scene and read until the final word on the final page. Study how you start and how you end your story. In these opening chapters you promise a journey for your readers. Does the journey come to a satisfying conclusion?

The stories I enjoy most have a resonance in their opening and final chapters – a connection, an echo. Did you feel that when you read your first and final chapters so close together? It's probably not appropriate for all books, but it's something that when I discover it, it adds to my reading experience.

In *Dark Parties*, my characters literally and figuratively start in the dark and end in the light. I also echo imagery of wings at the beginning and end. In the opening paragraph, my main character Neva thinks, 'My heart batters my ribs like a bird beating its wings against a glass cage.' The novel ends with the line, 'Hope gives my heart wings.' No reader may ever consciously recognize this, but I hope they will feel it.

Take what you've discovered in this chapter and make sure that your beginning and ending work together to maximize reader satisfaction.

Checklist

☐ **Are you pleased with how you start and end every chapter?**

You've made sure that each chapter uniquely draws us in and leaves us wanting more.

☐ **Have you hooked your reader from the opening page?**

If your opening isn't the best it can be, readers – starting with agents – will never discover the genius of the rest of your story. Those first pages open the door to your adventure. Make sure they represent you and your story to the best of your ability.

☐ **Have you provided a satisfying ending?**

Don't let fatigue undermine your ending by making it rushed or less well planned than the rest of your novel. The last moments you spend with readers will determine their overall satisfaction with the story. Don't flag in those final moments. Give your readers the ending they deserve so they will recommend your book and eagerly await your next one.

CHAPTER 11

The final polish

You've almost made it. This is the final push to polish your novel until it shines. This chapter covers what non-writers and novice writers – not you, obviously – may call *revising*. That's why non-writing friends and family are baffled that it has taken you twice or even three times as long to revise your novel as it did to write the blasted thing.

You know now that it's not enough to read and reread your novel from start to finish. This chapter provides several ways to proof your manuscript and shares many common errors to avoid. These final exercises ensure that your novel is ready to send to agents and editors – or self-publish if that's your aim. And we start with the very first words – your title.

Crafting the perfect title

Titles matter. It's the first thing a potential reader knows about your book. It can entice readers to pick it up or walk away.

Sometimes the title is what inspired the story. It may be the first words that you typed into the computer. Some writers need a title to get started. Others happily plod along with a working title, confident that the perfect title will spring to mind by the time they type *The End*.

Before you send your amazing novel into the real world – the novel that has taken you months, if not years, to write – find the best title you can. Not a title that's good enough, but one that will give your novel the best chance of surviving the slush pile.

Great titles are memorable, distinctive, intriguing, easy to say and clearly indicate the story you will tell. That said, they shouldn't give away plot twists or the ending. Create a title that targets the type of readers who will want to read your book. Don't have a funny title for your tragedy or an artsy title for your action-adventure.

Your title is a sales tool on the bookshop shelf. Does it make the right first impression? Also consider how your reader will see your title after they've finished the book. Will your reader have a new appreciation for the title then? Is there a richness to it, layers of meaning? This isn't a relevant issue for every book, but do think about how readers will view your title before and after they've read the book.

Here are a few quick-fire exercises to help you find the right title.

Exercise

Key words

Brainstorm key words and phrases that describe the plot, character, setting and theme of your book. Plug those words into a thesaurus and find more words.

Exercise

Bookshelf inspiration

Create a list of book titles you love. Ideally, some of these would be books in the same genre and for the same age as your reader. Why did these titles capture your imagination? Can you duplicate that spark in your title?

Title:
Why it works:

Title:
Why it works:

Title:
Why it works:

Exercise

Bookshop inspiration

Visit a bookshop and find books for the same age range and in the genre of your novel. You can do this online, but I find there's something about scanning the shelves and flipping through the book that inspires more than an Amazon search. Also, you can ask booksellers for titles they like and why. Make a list. What titles hook you? Can you hook your readers in the same way?

Title	Hook
1.	
2.	
3.	
4.	
5.	

Exercise

One line

Is there a line somewhere in your book that really sings? A moment that expresses the essential theme or heart of the story? What is it? Could it or a version of it be your title? The title of Annabel Pitcher's debut is drawn from the opening line of the novel – *My Sister Lives on the Mantelpiece*. It's intriguing and expresses what's at the heart of the story.

Exercise

Brainstorm titles

Now brainstorm as many titles as you can. Free-associate. Don't judge. Allow yourself to think of stupid and utterly ridiculous titles. This can sometimes lead to an unlikely but awesome title. At this stage, more is better.

1.

2.

3.

4.

5.

6.

7.

8.

9.

10.

11.

12.

13.

14.

15.

16.

17.

18.

19.

20.

Seeking help

And if you are still having trouble finding that perfect combination of words – and it really is a specific kind of genius that can encapsulate a book in a few words – get help. Could you brainstorm with someone who has read your work-in-progress? Sometimes a fresh perspective or someone who isn't so close to the work has a better chance of stepping back and seeing the big picture.

There are several title generators on the internet. You will have to input information about your novel, usually a high-level description, and it will spit out a list of options. If you tweak the way you've described your novel, it will generate even more. Use these to help you discover more words and inspire additional title suggestions. If you have a list of potential titles, but you're not sure which one is the best, share the list with your bookish friends. Which one stands out to them?

Exercise

Test your title

You think you've cracked the title code? Let's put it to the test with a title pop quiz.

1. Does it match the content of the book? You might like it because it's quirky or fresh or poetic, but if it doesn't match the story, don't use it. Your title should attract the right reader. If there's a disconnect, you may only disappoint readers. *Totally Deceased* by Sue Cunningham is a fantastic example of a title that sets the right tone. In two words, she's managed attitude and hinted at murder mystery.

2. Funny. Mystery. Romance. Literary. Is that communicated in your title? Mo O'Hara's *My Big Fat Zombie Goldfish* wonderfully communicates the quirky, funny nature of the book. Sophie Cameron's *Away with Words* is layered and poetic, just like the novel.

3. Is it memorable? Does it sound too much like any other book? Will it be confused with too many other titles? *Everyone Dies Famous in a Small Town* by Bonnie-Sue Hitchcock is a title like no other. It was longlisted for the Carnegie and purchased by me on the title alone.

4. Is it as short or as long as it needs to be? *Going Bovine* by Libba Bray and *The Girl Who Broke the Sea* by A. Connors are examples of intriguing titles that are exactly the length they need to be.

5. Say it out loud again and again – because if it gets published you will be saying it a lot! Is it easy to say with words that won't be confused at a glance?

When you finalise your title, search for your title on the internet and Amazon. It's difficult to find a title no one has used. Don't panic if someone has used your title, but do check if the book is for the same age range and genre as yours. And was it published in the last five years? If you answer yes to both questions, you may want to change it. If you find several books already out there with your title, start again.

And when at long last you've found the perfect title ... It's memorable and intriguing. It's exactly the right title to hook readers who will love your book. Job done, right? Probably not. If you are lucky enough to find an agent and a publisher, prepare yourself. Titles are subject to change. One agent told me she found that about 70 per cent of titles changed between submission and publication. But you should still do everything within your power to craft a standout title for your masterpiece. A poor or clunky title can put off editors and agents. Make sure your first impression is the best it can be.

That nagging feeling

Confront any nagging feelings you have about your story. It's that vague feeling that something just isn't working. Or maybe you know what's wrong but don't know how or don't want to face it. Maybe a character isn't behaving or there's a passage in your book that you aren't sure works. Now is the time to address whatever's bugging you. I've heard writers say they will leave things like this for an agent or editor to sort out, but agents and editors are really busy. If *they* have a nagging feeling about your manuscript, they may simply decide not to sign you. If you have a sneaking suspicion that there's still something wrong with your story, don't dismiss it. Ask someone you trust to read your book. After they've finished, ask them about what's been bothering you. (Don't tell them what you think is wrong before they read it. Don't put the issue in their head.) Did they think the same thing? Maybe they have suggestions for how to solve what you think isn't working.

The zing of satisfaction

When I read the final page of my manuscript – even when I'm reading it for what seems like the gazillionth time – I still get a zing of pride and satisfaction. Did you? I hope so. If not, why not? If you are not loving your manuscript for some reason, try to uncover the reason. If you aren't fascinated and engaged in your story, how can you possibly expect readers to be?

Line editing and proofreading

You've just finished reading your book for content – the big picture. Now is when we look at the granular detail of consistency, facts, spelling, grammar and punctuation. I don't think it's possible to check for everything in one reading of your manuscript; I plan to read through my novel several times and check for different things. If you have a good word processor, it will have flagged up any errors it has detected. But it's not perfect. Spell-check one final time.

Here are a few additional tricks to help you uncover any final irritating errors.

Read aloud

I like to read my book aloud at least once, but I've also recently discovered how helpful it can be to get your computer or your Kindle to read it aloud to you. Most word-processing software has a *Read Aloud* function. In Word, it's under the *Review* tab. Many e-readers have this function too. This is an investment of time, but the computer will read every word. You can even pick different voices and have it read at different speeds. It's amazing the number of times I discover either a missing word or the wrong word – *form* instead of *from*, for example.

Fact check

Double-check any facts you use. Often in a manuscript I will add a comment box with any research references – where I found a particular fact. This is the stage at which I check everything one last time. I had a story set in a seaside village, where one of my locations was the local fisherman's co-op. When I double-checked at the final stage, I learned that it had recently burned down. Because my story was set in the present, I had to change it.

It is always vital to revisit your story's chronology. You looked at this in the inventory exercise in Chapter 4, but do it again to make sure you haven't shifted dates or times since then.

Check for consistency

I mean consistency at every level. Here are a few examples of what I'm talking about. Do you refer to the same thing in the same way throughout your novel? I discovered that I referred to the Prime Minister's residence as No. 10 and Number Ten. Pick one and be consistent. Check if you've spelled first names and surnames the same. Your paragraph indentation, spacing, layout and font size should be the same throughout. No agent will reject you for wonky spacing or irregular indents, but this level of detail shows your professionalism.

Read out of order

This is where you'll think I've lost all touch with reality – if you don't already. I read my manuscript out of order. I've already read it once straight through for story, this is how I review my writing at a more micro level.

When we read and edit a manuscript, it makes sense to read it from beginning to end – starting with the first chapter and reading and reviewing through to the last. The only problem with this is that by the end of the novel, I'm fatigued. So once in my final review process, I start in the middle and read to the end and then read from the beginning to the middle. You will discover different things about your manuscript by reading it out of order.

I've also mixed up the chapters and read them out of order. And on short stories or when I'm sending sample chapters, I read the pages – sometimes even the paragraphs – out of order. I use a coloured pen and place a tick on the passages I've read and make sure every page or paragraph has a tick when I'm finished.

Final check

If you can stand it, set aside your manuscript for a month – at least two weeks. Don't look at it, and definitely don't work on it. I've spent months analysing my manuscript in all the ways I've outlined in this book. Before I send it out, I will try to read it as close to straight through in one sitting as I can. My aim is to duplicate the *reader's* experience of my novel. (I know that's impossible, but do give it a go.)

- Really concentrate. Most adults have an attention span of 45 minutes. Take breaks when fatigued. Consider changing your location: if you wrote the story in your office, read it in a café, for example.

- Change the font or type size and read a printed manuscript or read it on your e-reader. The words on the page will shift, and I promise you will find a few things that you need to fix.

- If you have printed your manuscript, use a sheet of paper or ruler to cover material not yet proofed. Point with your finger to read one word at a time.

- Scrutinize homonyms – there/their/they're, here/hear, two/too/to, etc.

- Keep a list of your most common errors and check for those. I have a document on my computer titled, *Sara's Common Errors*. Every time an editor, copy-editor or proofreader sends feedback on my manuscript, I note what they've found and add it to this list. I don't make those mistakes again. (I usually make new ones.) What are your common errors?

If you can, have someone else proofread it. But at this stage in the process, be clear what you are asking them to do. Do you want comments on the story or just grammar and punctuation?

The final proofread

If you've made significant edits at any of the proofreading stages, take a deep breath and read the novel one final time. No, this is it. I mean it. I always tell myself that I've spent hundreds of hours on this book already, so what's 10, 20 or 30 more?

On my recent work-in-progress, my agent had given me a few minor notes. Once I addressed them, I thought that maybe I didn't need to read it again. I mean, I'd paid careful attention when I was making the changes. Another reading was overkill. I texted my WhatsApp group of published writer friends to just double-check that it was okay for me to send the manuscript back to my agent without another read. Nearly every one of them immediately replied NO! I needed to read it one more time. I did. I found a few errors, fixed them and was then more confident when I sent it back to my agent.

When to stop

One of the most difficult things about revision is knowing when to stop. Some writers can get stuck in an endless cycle of revision. There's always room for improvement, right? Well, yes, I suppose that's true. But sometime fear of failure can keep us from sending our darling manuscript into the world to be judged. This takes nerves of steel, determination and maybe a stiff drink.

I know my manuscript is ready for the world when I tinker at the line-editing stage. I make miniscule improvements which make a scene different but not better. There can also be a point at which we overthink our stories and can sometimes make them worse. If you find yourself stuck in this endless revision loop, set the novel aside for a few weeks. Then when you pick it up again, interrogate each edit you want to make. Is it making it better? Also analyse why you are continuing to edit. If you believe in your gut that something still isn't working, by all means pick up your red pen and get back to work. But if your gut is telling you to stop, then listen to it.

Stop and celebrate! You've done it!
You can think of no way to improve your manuscript.

Checklist

☐ **Is your title memorable, distinctive, intriguing and easy to say? Does it clearly indicate the story you will tell?**

If you don't think you've nailed it, ask for help from a writer friend. Brainstorm with them. Keep working until you find a title that works for your story.

☐ **Are you satisfied that: your idea is original and publishable? Your voice is distinctive? Your plot hangs together? The pace of your story will keep readers reading? Your characters are engaging and three-dimensional? And the atmosphere maximizes the setting and your reader's experience?**

These are big things. Take a moment to really analyse each of these aspects of your novel. Do you have any questions or niggles? If fatigue has set in, take a break from your novel and come back again in a month and ask yourself these big questions again. Make sure you aren't giving up or fed up with your story. Try to step back and assess your novel critically one last time.

☐ **Are you happy with every page, paragraph, line and word?**

When you give it that one final read, you should feel a deep sense of satisfaction. All of the puzzle pieces have fallen into place and you are happy with your novel at every level. You can think of no way to improve it. Is that how you feel?

The challenging thing – if you want to be traditionally published – is that you work independently to make your manuscript the best it can be, but you will have to embrace collaboration at various points. If you are lucky enough to find an agent and/or an editor, they will give you feedback. Your revision process – albeit a much shorter period – will start again.

I hope that by completing many of these exercises and interrogating your novel at a macro and micro level, you will have learned about yourself as a writer, which will shorten the revision process for future novels.

CHAPTER 12

Ready for the world

You have a draft that's ready to show the world – the vital first step on your path to publication. But it's only the initial hurdle. I'm going to talk a bit about why you need an agent, the type of agent to look for and give you a few ideas about how to pull together your submissions packet. I also want to leave you with a few final thoughts, things I've learned on my own rocky and wonderful writerly journey.

Why you need an agent

You can certainly go it alone and reach out to editors directly, though most publishers of fiction will only accept submissions via an agent. Here's what agents provide …

- *A business partner.* Publishing is a tough business. As writers, we focus on the creative side, but don't forget that it's a business. There are politics, unwritten rules, trends, personalities, local and global markets, and much more to consider. Having an agent gives you a smart, savvy business partner, someone by your side for the highs and lows. They focus on the business of publishing so you can focus on writing the best book you can – again and again.

- *An editorial expert.* Most agents will work editorially with an author before they send out a manuscript. They offer authors advice based not only on their publishing expertise – many agents are former editors – but also on market trends. In short, agents know what will give your book the best chance of selling in the current publishing climate.

- *Market knowledge.* An agent's job is not just to understand the current state of children's publishing, but also to know the personalities of the real-life people who acquire books. They know what specific editors like and don't like, who's on their lists and what they've just purchased. It's impossible for a writer to acquire this knowledge and develop relationships with the many, many editors who publish fiction.

- *A stamp of approval.* Signing with an agent means an expert has invested time in you. You can have more confidence with someone in your corner, and editors will have more confidence in your work, too.

- *Faster response from editors.* If you send your manuscript to an editor at a specific publishing house, it will be placed on what used to be called the slush pile – and now more politely called a to-read pile.

But it is a huge stack! Most editors receive hundreds of unsolicited manuscripts a month. It can take them months to respond – if they respond at all. Typically editors will read and respond to agents much faster than to individual writers. Read publisher submission guidelines carefully. Most publishers do not accept unsolicited manuscripts direct from authors.

- ***Experience in negotiation and contracts.*** If you want to look solely at the bottom line, an agent is likely to land you a better advance than you could secure on your own. Agents understand the market – what's a realistic advance and royalty. I hate talking about money. With my first book, I had no idea whether the amount they offered was too low. My agent did, though, and made sure I received a great deal.

- ***More leverage.*** Agents have more bargaining power than one author. They represent many authors. Maybe one or more of their authors has been acquired by the publisher who's making an offer. Agents know what to ask for, when to walk away and which battles to pick.

- ***Global reach.*** Agents can sell more rights. It would be difficult, if not impossible, for an author to approach and negotiate deals with publishers in other countries. Most authors without agents will sell all the rights to a book. Agents might hold back some global, audio or media rights. Thanks to my agent, to date the most lucrative deal I signed was with a German publisher. (I don't speak German but do love their pretzels and their incredible culture of reading.) My agent partnered with another in-house agent who knew the German market and was able to find a wonderful publisher and negotiate a two-book deal.

Choosing an agent or editor

Whether you plan to approach agents first or go directly to editors, be thoughtful about who to target. The relationships between agent/editor/ writer are important ones. Think about what type of partnership you want. Do you want an agent who provides lots of editorial feedback? Do you want an agent from a big agency or an agent who has formed their own agency? Similarly, would you prefer an editor at a big or indie publisher? A well-known or hungry young editor? Each has its pros and cons.

Here are a few questions to ask yourself before you draw up your list of prospective agents or editors:

List, in order, the most important and least important traits you are looking for in an agent or editor. I didn't have any strong feelings about big or small agencies. I wanted someone who would support me editorially and offer feedback on a completed manuscript but also at the early stages of a new project, when an idea was starting to take shape. I wanted someone who understood me and my book. I also wanted to see their passion for my project and the industry.

What are your career goals? Is this book the only book you intend to write? Or do you hope for a long, multi-book career? If you plan to write more books, do you want to write in the same genre and for the same age range or do you want an agent who can sell picture books and books for adults too?

Your responses will help you find the best agent and editor for you. Some of the most comprehensive lists of agents and editors can be found in the *Children's Writers' & Artists' Yearbook* and the *Writers' & Artists' Yearbook*. It's published annually and has up-to-date contact information as well as tips and advice for writers and illustrators. The key to finding the perfect agent/editor match is to do your research and be professional. Look for agents who represent the type of fiction you are writing. Then dig deeper. Most agents have an internet and social media presence. Review their websites. Research the writers on their lists. You need to fit in, but you can't be writing something too similar to something they've recently sold. Search for blogs, articles and Q&As with the agents and editors who interest you. A quick scroll through their social media might also give you clues about what they are looking for.

We'll talk next about creating your submissions package, but first you will need to create a list of the agents or editors you plan to target. Read their submissions policies – and then send them exactly what they want in the way they want to receive it. Don't send a blanket email query to every agent and editor you can find.

Preparing your submissions package

Your submissions package is your calling card to agents and editors. Make sure you are giving yourself and your work the best opportunity with these gatekeepers.

It should include:

- A cover letter.
- A synopsis of your book – ideally, one page and no more than two.
- Most likely, the first three chapters of your novel – though some agents may prefer that you send a set number of words from the novel's beginning or the entire manuscript. Check out their submission guidelines and always follow their instructions.

Cover letter

You can search online for cover letter templates and examples, but here's my step-by-step guide for creating a professional letter.

1. Personalize the email. No generic greetings. Use the recipient's name, and make sure you are spelling it correctly. I can't tell you how many people email me with a greeting *Hi Sarah* – with an h. I don't really mind, but double-check the spelling before you hit send.

2. Each of the following should be a short, straightforward paragraph:
   - Get to the point. You are looking for representation for your [*total word count*]-word [*age range – 5+, 7+, middle grade, young adult or adult*] [*genre*] novel, titled [*title*]. Then hit them with your short pitch. Does the one you created in Chapter 1 still best represent your novel? You want your pitch to grab their attention so they have to read on. If there's series potential, say this – not that you have 20 books written, even if you do. In the current publishing climate, editors don't routinely offer multiple book deals to debut authors. Publishers often want to see how the first book sells before offering another contract.

- Next give them your paragraph blurb – a few sentences that capture the essence of the story, but doesn't give away too much. Look at the blurbs on book jackets for great examples. Yours should be a four- or five-sentence paragraph.

- Now, add a line or two about why you think this person would be the best agent or editor for you and your book. Show your research. You read and loved a book by one of her/his/their authors and your book is like that in some way. You heard them speak at a conference or read an interview online, and something they said made you believe they would connect with your work.

- Share your inspiration or reason for writing this book – if that's interesting and appropriate. Not: *I had the idea in the bath after my third glass of wine.* But: *this story was inspired by a protest I attended,* if it's a book about the issue you were protesting or about civil disobedience. Perhaps you have an expertise in some aspect of your novel and/or you have a significant social media presence for something related to your novel or to writing in general. If your book covers any of the areas we discussed in Chapter 7, it's helpful for agents and editors to know your story is based on lived experience. If there's no interesting tale behind the story or it's not based on your experience, omit this section.

- Add any writing credentials or job experience if relevant and/or interesting. You want to demonstrate that you are a professional and take your writing seriously. You are a scientist, and your story is about a young scientist. Not *I'm a nurse, and my story is about unicorns and puppies.* Definitely mention if you have been published in any significant way. Mention if you are a member of any professional writing organizations, such as the Society of Children's Book Writers and Illustrators (SCBWI), if you have a degree in creative writing or have won or been shortlisted for any awards or prizes. Don't worry if you don't have that quirky story about your reason for writing or an impressive job or expertise. I didn't. But if you have it, use it.

3. Then close with a simple *looking forward to hearing from you*. Make sure you include your full name and any contact information, such as a mobile phone number.

Synopsis and sample chapters

If you've worked your way through the exercises in this book, your synopsis and sample chapters should be good to go. Ask a writer friend or two – individuals who don't know your novel – to read your cover letter and your synopsis to make sure they make sense.

A few don'ts

I've covered the dos for your submissions package, but here are a few don'ts. For the past seven years, I've hosted SCBWI's agent party for the British Isles. Here's what I've learned from interviewing several agents during that time:

- Don't send your novel out too soon. We can all hear that ticking clock. We've finished our novel, and we need to send it out RIGHT NOW. I've mentioned this already, but I'll repeat: set your novel aside for at least a few weeks and then read it again before sending it out. Submit it out only when you are sure that you can think of no other way to revise it. You get one shot for each book with agents and editors. They remember what they've read.

- Proofread your submission email many, many times. If you are cutting and pasting, double-check to make sure you've customized each message for each agent/editor.

- No gimmicks. Someone sent an agent an oven mitt because their manuscript was 'too hot to handle'. You don't want your submissions package to stand out for anything other than your brilliant idea and gorgeous prose.

- Don't tell agents or editors about their jobs or the industry. *As you know, llamas are hot right now*, for example. By the time you send it – and definitely in the time it would take to publish your book, llamas will be old news. Once when I was an intern and asked to review an agent's slush pile, one letter said, 'Sit down and pay attention because my novel will change your life.' It didn't.

- Don't mention that your friends, family, or pupils liked your story. The people in your life want to please you, so they will be kind. They also might not have the language or confidence to tell you what's not working. It's not an unbiased or professional critique of your work, and it certainly won't impress an agent or editor.

And do be patient! Agents and editors receive hundreds if not thousands of queries a year. It could take months for an agent to respond to you. After three months, it's acceptable to follow up with a politely worded email, asking if they received it.

Next steps

Agents and editors who are interested will most likely want to meet you virtually or in real life before they make an offer. Come prepared to talk about your book, but also about you! I cringe when asked, 'Tell me something about yourself.' There's a fine line between being confident and bragging. On the opposite end, you also don't want to say, 'I'm just a small-town girl from Indiana; there's nothing special about me.' They are investing in you. Why are you worth their investment?

They may want to know the story behind the story. Why did you write the book? In Chapter 1, we covered your intention – why you felt compelled to write the story. Tell them that. They also will want to see if you have more than one book in you. Come prepared with a few ideas for future books. These can be prequels or sequels to the story you are pitching, but have other ideas, too. I'd write no more than a few paragraphs or a page for each idea – just the pitch and the blurb.

Develop a list of questions to ask them. Yes, they are interviewing you, but it's equally important for you to interview them. How much editorial work do they do with writers? What do they think are your novel's strengths? What are its weaknesses?

Above all, be professional and respectful. It's a two-way street – both you and the agent or editor need to be happy. Both you and your agent or editor will succeed together.

It's easy to get disheartened – a no from agents and from editors comes quickly. A yes will take time. But all you need is that one agent and one editor to see the genius of you and your story.

Never give up!

Sure, *now* I've had ten novels published with wonderful publishers such as Little, Brown, Orion and Scholastic. But not so long ago, I was right where you are. Okay, not exactly where you are, but I know what it's like to have a manuscript that you've given your blood, sweat and tears – and to want to be published *so* badly. It's been a weird and wonderful ride. There have been some amazing highs: the first time I saw my book on a bookshop shelf: and some crushing lows, manuscripts that never found a publisher. I offer three words that I hope will help you on your writerly way.

Tenacity. Every writer is unique, their journeys varied and valuable. From the age of eight, I wanted to write stories. But growing up, I mistakenly thought that an ordinary child from a small town in the Midwestern United States couldn't be a writer. I was wrong. I started taking my writing seriously in 1994. After seventeen years of writing, revising and rejection, I received my first book deal. Getting published can be a rollercoaster, but don't give up.

Collaboration. Being a traditionally published author means collaboration. Find professionals – an agent and editor – you trust and respect. And listen to them. That doesn't mean agreeing to every edit, but being open to letting others into your writing process. And pick your battles. I'm lucky to have worked with some of the best in the business. I listened and learned. I signed my first book deal with Alvina Ling at Little, Brown because before she made an offer, she gave me editorial notes. Her keen observations and editorial prowess nailed what wasn't working in *Dark Parties*. She made it a better book and me a better writer.

Joy! When my first book was published, I was a nervous wreck. Yes, I'd achieved something I'd dreamed about since I was a child. But in addition to the fear of what people would think of my book, I had blogs to write, schools to visit and the 24-7 world of social media. My lovely husband sat me down and said that I had achieved something few people ever do, something I'd always wanted – and yet I wasn't enjoying it. He was right. From then on, I decided to enjoy every minute of this crazy ride for as long as it lasts.

If the stars align and your book finds a publishing home, wonderful. If you are on award lists, brilliant. If you become a bestseller, amazing! But if not, celebrate that you've done a rare and brave thing by committing your unique and wonderful story to the page – and you've done the hard work of revising and editing your novel to make it the best it can be.

Keep writing. Keep learning. Keep improving. And keep the faith.

RESOURCES AND REFERENCES

Books about writing and editing

Bell, James Scott. *Plot & Structure: Techniques and Exercises for Crafting a Plot that Grips Readers From Start to Finish* (Penguin Publishing Group, 2004)

Bell, James Scott. *Revision and Self-Editing for Publication: Techniques for Transforming Your First Draft into a Novel that Sells* (Penguin Publishing Group, 2012)

Bell, James Scott. *Voice: The Secret Power of Great Writing* (Compendium Press, 2015)

Bell, James Scott. *Write Your Novel from the Middle: A New Approach for Plotters, Pantsers and Everyone in Between* (Compendium Press, 2014)

Browne, Renni and Dave King. *Self-Editing for Fiction Writers: How to Edit Yourself Into Print* (HarperCollins, 2004)

Burroway, Janet. *Writing Fiction: A Guide to Narrative Craft* (Longman, 2000)

Cron, Lisa. *Story Genius: How to Use Brain Science to Go Beyond Outlining and Write a Riveting Novel* (Ten Speed Press, 2016)

Iglesias, Karl. *Writing for Emotional Impact: Advanced Dramatic Techniques to attract, engage, and fascinate the reader from beginning to end* (WingSpan Press, 2005)

King, Stephen. *On Writing: A Memoir of the Craft* (Hodder & Stoughton, 2001)

Lukeman, Noah. *The Plot Thickens: 8 Ways to Bring Fiction to Life* (St. Martin's Griffin, 2002)

McKee, Robert. *Story: Substance, Structure, Style, and the Principles of Screenwriting* (Regan Books, 1997)

Pattison, Darcy. *Novel Metamorphosis: Uncommon Ways to Revise* (Mims House, 2008)

Snyder, Blake. *Save the Cat! Strikes Back: More Trouble for Screenwriters to Get Into . . . & Out Of* (Save the Cat! Press, 2009)

Children's Writers' & Artists' Yearbook (Bloomsbury, July annually)

Writers' & Artists' Yearbook (Bloomsbury, July annually)

Recommended fiction

These are titles mentioned in the text, listed alphabetically by author surname. Publication date is that of the British first edition. Numbers after each title are page numbers in this book where it is referred to.

M.T. Anderson, *Feed* (Walker Books, 2003) 199

Malorie Blackman, *Noughts & Crosses* (Doubleday, 2001) 108

Adam Blade, *Beast Quest* (Orchard Books, 2007–) 14

Libba Bray, *Going Bovine* (Delacorte Press, 2009) 199, 201, 225

Anna Brooke, *Monster Bogey* (Chicken House, 2023) 131

Sophie Cameron, *Away with Words* (Little Tiger Press, 2023) 225

Suzanne Collins, *The Hunger Games* (Scholastic, 2008) 12, 41

A. Connors, *The Girl Who Broke the Sea* (Scholastic, 2023) 225

Frank Cottrell-Boyce, *Millions* (Macmillan, 2004) 48

Dave Cousins, *Fifteen Days Without a Head* (Oxford University Press, 2012) 63

Sue Cunningham, *Totally Deceased* (Scholastic, 2023) 225

Roald Dahl, *Charlie and the Chocolate Factory* (Allen & Unwin, 1964) 12, 73

A.M. Dassu, *Fight Back* (Scholastic, 2022) 63

Benjamin Dean, *The Secret Sunshine Project* (Simon & Schuster, 2022) 198

Jennifer Donnelly, *A Gathering Light* (UK) (Bloomsbury, 2004) 13, 98, 199

Tia Fisher, *Crossing the Line* (Hot Key Books, 2023) 83

Sally Gardner, *Maggot Moon* (Hot Key Books, 2012) 84

Candy Gourlay, *Wild Song* (David Fickling Books, 2023) 36

Michael Grant, *Gone* (Egmont, 2009) 199

Simon James Green, *Noah Can't Even* (Scholastic, 2017) 13

Bonnie-Sue Hitchcock, *Everyone Dies Famous in a Small Town* (Faber & Faber, 2021) 225

Danielle Jawando, *When Our Worlds Collided* (Simon & Schuster, 2022) 83

Jennifer Killick, *Dread Wood* (Farshore, 2022) 57

Stephen King, *Under the Dome* (Hodder & Stoughton, 2009) 17

Katie Kirby, *The Extremely Embarrassing Life of Lottie Brooks* (Puffin, 2021) 83

Alice Kulpers, *Life on the Refrigerator Door* (Macmillan, 2007) 83

Ingrid Law, *Savvy* (Puffin, 2008) 199, 201

Harper Lee, *To Kill a Mockingbird* (Heinemann, 1960) 26

David Levithan, *Every Day* (Electric Monkey, 2013) 57

Terri Libenson, *Invisible Emmie* (Balzer + Bray, 2017) 83–4

Barry Lyga, *I Hunt Killers* (Little, Brown and Company, 2012) 198, 201

Tracey Mathias, *Silence is Also a Lie* (Scholastic, 2020) 60

Daisy Meadows, *Rainbow Magic* (Orchard Books, 2003–) 12

Sienna Mercer, *My Sister the Vampire* (Egmont, 2009–16) 18

Stephanie Meyer, *Twilight* (Little, Brown and Company, 2005) 14

Patrick Ness, *The Knife of Never Letting Go* (Walker Books, 2008) 20, 198, 201

Mo O'Hara, *My Big Fat Zombie Goldfish* (Square Fish, 2014) 20, 225

Tọlá Okogwu, *Onyeka and the Academy of the Sun* (Simon & Schuster, 2022) 58

Serena Patel, *Anisha, Accidental Detective* (Usborne, 2020) 13

Dav Pilkey, *Captain Underpants* (Scholastic, 2000–15) 63

Annabel Pitcher, *My Sister Lives on the Mantelpiece* (Indigo, 2011) 222

Philip Reeve, *Mortal Engines* (Scholastic, 2001) 198, 201

Dashe Roberts, *The Bigwoof Conspiracy* (Nosy Crow, 2020) 199

J.K. Rowling, *Harry Potter* (Bloomsbury, 1997–2007) 18, 62, 73

Louis Sachar, *Holes* (Bloomsbury, 2000) 212

Rex Stone, *Dinosaur Club* (DK, 2022–) 20

Ashley Thorpe, *The Boy to Beat the Gods* (Usborne, 2024) 14

J.T. Williams, *The Lizzie and Belle Mysteries: Drama and Danger* (Farshore, 2022) 12

Index of exercises

Acknowledgements

I'm still a work-in-progress with so many people who have supported me and shaped my story. I'll start with the most important – my husband Paul. He gives me the confidence to share my stories with the world and encourages me as we continue on this crazy publishing rollercoaster. I would have never achieved my dream of being a published author without him!

A huge thanks to my agent Jenny Savill and the team at Andrew Nurnberg Associates. She's been an amazing business partner, trusted councillor, and friend. I'm thankful for her continued support at every stage of my writing career.

To the team at Bloomsbury for seeing the promise in this book and for their incredible editorial guidance. They've made me and this book better. Thanks, Alysoun Owen and Alice Rose. And to copy-editor Lisa Carden for brilliantly editing a book about editing. Thanks to the three of you for your questions and eagle eyes. Thank you to Catherine Lutman for her text design and for the teams at Writers and Artists (James Rennoldson, Clare Povey and Amelia Brown) and Bloomsbury who have promoted and sold this book.

Also a sincere thanks to the 'other' Sara – Sara O'Connor. You are a true friend, always offering a critical editorial eye, welcome advice and a listening ear.

To the team at Storymix for inspiring me every day and demonstrating the magic of inclusivity in the workplace and on the page. A special thanks to Jasmine Richards, Ashley Thorpe, Simran Sandhu, Eva Wong and Beth Cox for reading and responding to my chapter on sensitivity/authenticity and offering me wonderful advice.

And to my 'Forest' Writer Friends. We connected in real life and then through the pandemic on an app that let us virtually write together nearly every day. I'm lucky to have a group of talented authors to call my friends – Marie Basting, Rosie Best, Peter Bunzl, Gail Doggett,

Candy Gourlay, Tracey Mathias, Lou Minns, Kimberley Pauley and Sue Wallman. Thanks for responding to my random questions and offering support when it was really needed.

Thanks to my beta readers – Dave Powell, Sue Wallman, Marie Basting, Lou Minns and Richard Parker. They read an early draft of this book and offered ideas and edits big and small to improve the book. I can't thank them enough for taking time out of their busy writerly lives to offer advice.

And thanks to you for reading. Here's wishing you joy in your writing, productivity in your editing – and ultimately satisfied readers of your stories.

Author biography

Sara Grant writes and edits fiction for children and teens. *Dark Parties*, her first young adult novel, won the Society of Children's Book Writers and Illustrators Crystal Kite Award for Europe. Ten of her books have been traditionally published, for a range of ages and across several genres. As an editor of series fiction, she has worked on fifteen different series and edited nearly 100 books. She consults with Storymix (storymix.co.uk), an inclusive fiction studio, helping develop exciting and engaging stories with children of colour at the heart. She has taught master's courses on writing for children/teens at Goldsmiths, University of London and at the University of Winchester and has run writing workshops in the US, UK and Europe. She co-founded *Undiscovered Voices*, which has launched the writing careers of more than a hundred authors and illustrators, who have collectively published more than 400 children's books (undiscoveredvoices.com). She was shortlisted for *The Bookseller* Freelancer of the Year Award 2024.

Sara was born and raised in Washington, Indiana. She graduated from Indiana University with degrees in journalism and psychology, and later gained a master's degree in creative and life writing at Goldsmiths, University of London. She lives in London.

Bluesky @AuthorSaraGrant.bsky.social
Substack saragrant1.substack.com
LinkedIn Sara Grant
X @authorsaragrant
Website www.sara-grant.com